GLOBAL AIR
★ TROUBLE ★
SHOOTERS

Crash at
CANNIBAL
VALLEY

JERRY JENKINS

CRASH IN CANNIBAL VALLEY
Book 1

published by Multnomah Books
a part of the Questar publishing family

© 1996 by Jerry B. Jenkins

International Standard Book Number: 0-88070-970-7

Cover illustration by Laura Smith

Printed in the United States of America.

For information:
Questar Publishers, Inc.
Post Office Box 1720
Sisters, Oregon 97759

Library of Congress Cataloging-in-Publication Data
Jenkins, Jerry B.
    Crash at Cannibal Valley / by Jerry Jenkins.
        p.   cm. -- (Global Air Troubleshooters ; #1)
    Summary: When their small plane goes down in an area in Indonesia inhabited by
cannibals, Spitfire and his family have their faith in God tested as they fight to survive
against all odds.
    ISBN 0-88070-970-7 (alk. paper)
    [1. Cannibalism--Fiction. 2. Survival--Fiction. 3. Indonesia-adventurers--Fiction.]
    I. Title. II. Series: Jenkins, Jerry B. Global Air Troubleshooters ; #1.
    PZ7.J4138Cr   1997   96-30713
    [Fic]--dc20   CIP
                                                                  AC

96 97 98 99 00 01 02 03 — 10 9 8 7 6 5 4 3 2 1

To Dallas, Chad, and Michael
May you remain ever young at heart.

CHAPTER 1

Misery in Mukluk

Chad Michaels bounded out of Mukluk Middle School in northern Alaska. He ran as fast as he could despite huge boots, down-filled snow pants, mittens, and hooded parka.

He and his sixth-grade buddies usually engaged in daily snowball fights against the seventh graders. Chad hated these fights. Today's snowball fight might have ruined his entire day, but he had two special things to look forward to that afternoon, and that's what he thought about as he ran out into the snow.

The winter sun set early in Mukluk, so the whole school was let out for recess before lunch every day. That meant there were just too many kids to watch at once, and the boys could get away with breaking the no-snowball rule. Besides, these guys had been snowball fighting for so long, they knew where to play without getting caught.

Chad hadn't even had time to stop and scoop up a ball of his own when he saw Rusty Testor, his least favorite seventh grader, standing a few feet away, a huge snowball in his palm. The icy wind stung Chad's exposed cheeks as he sprinted for all he was worth, but the bigger, older Testor had the angle on him and was closing fast.

Rusty had a gap-toothed, freckle-faced grin that gave Chad nightmares. *I'd love to pop him, just once,* Chad thought. He imagined himself rushing Testor, driving his head into the bigger boy's stomach, and knocking the wind right out of him. That's what his friends would do.

But not me, Chad thought as he ran. *They're right. I'm a wimp.*

Chad headed for the highest, deepest drift he could find, planning to hurtle over it and fight back from the other side. But from the corner of his eye he saw Testor draw back his throwing arm. Chad mistimed his leap over the snowdrift and left the ground too early. He spread his arms and legs, but instead of flying over the top to safety, he flopped face-first into the side of the drift.

As he turned to see if any of his friends would help, Rusty's snowball smacked his cheekbone and drove ice and water into his ear and eye. He wanted to cry, but he would never do that. It was bad enough he was a klutz; he wasn't going to be a baby too. At least he wouldn't show it if he was.

Chad turned to see what was coming next, and there stood Rusty, scooping more ammo from about ten feet away. Several other seventh graders joined in, grinning just like Rusty. Chad squatted to make his own snowball, but all that did was make the older kids move faster. He sat, covering his face with his arms and drawing up his knees to protect himself as the fusillade pummeled him.

Chad wondered where his friends were. Here was the perfect opportunity to charge the seventh graders from the rear, while they were all occupied with him. He had sacrificed himself, not on purpose of course, but the least he expected was that his comrades would take advantage of the situation.

But they just stood outside the circle of older kids, looking at him in disgust.

"You're too easy," Rusty said. "Go hide somewhere."

Chad wanted to charge him, to throw ice balls at him. But he knew what would happen. He would get no help, and he would be a sitting duck once again. He stood, shoulders sagging, hands at his sides, as the seventh graders turned their attention to his friends. They would put up a better fight, which was more fun for the seventh graders than terrorizing Chad.

When they trudged back into school for lunch, one of Chad's friends caught up with him. "What's the deal, Michaels? Every day it's the same thing! You're big enough, you're strong enough, you're fast enough You're as good at basketball as anybody in the class. But outside you're like a pansy."

How was he supposed to answer that? He didn't know himself. Chad just shook his head as he peeled off his snow gear. He wouldn't let anything ruin this special day, even if he wasn't the rugged outdoorsman that most of the boys at Mukluk Middle School seemed to be. They fished and hunted and camped. They hiked and knew all about animals and plants. He had nothing against that, and his father had taught him as much as anyone else knew about the outdoors. The truth was, he just wasn't good at all that stuff.

Chad would rather sit at his computer, surfing the Internet or maintaining his files on his favorite pro and college sports teams in the lower forty-eight states. He loved downloading scores and statistics in the morning before school; because of the time difference, all the results from the night before were already listed on the news and wire services. No one in the school knew as much as he did about sports.

His parents had encouraged him on the computer, because they saw what it had done for his schoolwork.

After lunch Chad's teacher, Mrs. Wright, called the class to attention. "For the third straight time, I'm happy to announce that Chad Michaels is our student of the month." She added, "Congratulations, Chad," as most of the boys shook their heads and grimaced, while several of the girls turned and smiled at him. Chad knew the guys were jealous, but there were days when he wished he were an average student who could hit Rusty Testor between the eyes with a snowball.

"And," Mrs. Wright said, "Chad has two things to share with the class. Chad?"

The boys groaned again, one of them muttering, "Is this where we get to hear about his dad the hero again? Does he still call you Spitfire, Michaels?"

Mrs. Wright shushed them as Chad rose to speak. "Well, first, my sister Kate is going to come and speak to our class today, in about half an hour."

"Is it true you two were born in the same year?" someone blurted.

"It's true," Chad said. "I was born in January and she was born in December."

"So for a little while each year you two are the same age."

"Sort of, but of course she's in fifth grade."

"We'll let Kate tell us what she's going to share when she comes in," Mrs. Wright said. "But what else—"

"Radios, of course," one of the girls said. "She knows everything there is about radios."

Chad nodded. "Course," he said. "She knows more'n my dad."

"I knew *he* would come up," a boy said.

"Now that's enough," Mrs. Wright said. "I *do* want Chad to tell us what's so special about today, besides his sister coming to our class, and it does relate to his father. Chad?"

"Well, the best part is, Kate and I get to leave school about an hour and a half early today. The peace-keeping mission is over in the Middle East, and my dad landed near Washington, D.C., several hours ago. He should be in Anchorage soon, and then he'll fly here. My mother is going to pick us up and we'll meet him at the airport."

"Did he kill anybody over there?" someone shouted.

"I don't know," Chad said. "He could have. He flies—"

"Fighter planes; yeah, we know."

Chad sat back down, knowing again that his friends were just jealous. None of their fathers did anything as fun and exciting as his dad did. Even when he wasn't being called into duty by the Air Force, he flew charter flights all over Alaska, Canada, the northeastern United States, and even the Pacific. He owned his own company—he called it Yukon Do It—which included ten planes and employed several pilots.

The other kids could mutter all they wanted and make fun of him, but Chad knew they wished their dads were as daring as his. The school assemblies that Bruce Michaels spoke at each year were always the most popular and talked about. And when Chad's class took a field trip to his dad's hangar, and the kids got to take rides in one of the small charter planes, Chad lived for days on the attention. For a while, some of the kids even called Chad Spitfire like his dad did. Chad loved it when his dad called him Spitfire. Mr. Michaels had told him a Spitfire was a World War II plane that could be quick and deadly. "And that's you," his dad often said.

Chad was always amazed at what his sister could do. She didn't even seem nervous when she arrived with her radios and oscillators and gave her little demonstration. A bit shorter and thinner than Chad, she had his blond hair and green eyes, and it wasn't unusual for people to ask if they were twins.

After a few interruptions from the class clowns, Kate quickly won them over with her knowledge of the history of the discovery of radio waves, and her explanation of how quickly the technology had grown, even in just the last five years. "You know," she said, "that television signals are really just high frequency radio waves. Some day we'll be wearing TV's on our wrists and looking at each other while we talk."

She also told about her recent trip with her father to an Asian radio manufacturing plant, and all she had seen and done there. When she finished she received loud applause and cheering. "I have to get going now," she said, smiling, "because in about half an hour, my mom—"

"We know, we know!" some boys hollered. "We've heard all about it!"

Kate blushed as she packed up her things.

Chad and Kate squabbled as much as any other brother and sister, but now he sat beaming. He was proud of her, and while he might not admit that to her, it felt good. He was glad she was his sister.

Chad found it hard to concentrate on anything during the next half-hour. He had his stuff arranged and was ready to go. His dad had been gone six weeks now. It had been longer the time before, and he *had* shot down an enemy plane that time.

Chad's mother was good about not showing her worry. They prayed for Dad every night, of course, and Chad knew his mom missed Dad most of all. But she didn't cry or talk about the danger all the time. She said there was just as much danger when he flew his charter flights, and they weren't going to waste their lives away worrying about things that may never happen.

Chad stared at his watch, trying to make the time go faster. The seconds seemed to tick like minutes. At two o'clock he was to go by Kate's classroom and walk with her to the office where his mother would meet them, sign them out, and then they'd head for the airstrip, forty-five minutes away.

Finally his watch showed two o'clock sharp. With a nod from Mrs. Wright, Chad quietly left the room. "Say 'hi' to your dad for us," someone whispered. He nodded. He could even put up with Rusty Testor on a day like this.

"So, how'd I do, Chad?" Kate asked as they made their way to the office.

"It was all right," Chad said.

"Just all right?" she said. "Really? Just all right?"

"You were great, of course," Chad said reluctantly. Why couldn't he ever tell her how he really felt? What would be wrong with that?

"You sound like you'd be happier if I'd made a fool of myself," she said.

"Nah," he said. "You did good."

"*Well,* you mean."

"Yeah, you did well."

Chad was surprised his mother was not already at the office. He and Kate peeked outside at the parking lot to watch for her while the receptionist took a call. "Kids," she said then, "your mother's been delayed. It'll be a little while longer."

Chad squinted as he wondered. "Was that her on the phone?"

"Um, no. But they told me she has been detained a bit."

"Detained?" Kate said.

"Yeah, you know—held up, delayed."

"I know what it means," Kate said. "But who told you that?"

The receptionist looked nervous. "I didn't catch his name," she said.

"Listen," Chad said, "my dad's supposed to touch down in an hour, and we're supposed to be there waiting for him. He'll worry if we're not—"

"It won't be long," the receptionist said, "before we'll know something definite."

"About what?" Chad said. "Who was on the phone?"

"I just take the messages, kids. I don't explain them. Your mother has been delayed, so you might just as well take a seat and wait."

"For how long?"

"I don't know!"

"Well, what did they say, whoever they were?"

"You know as much as I do," she said, turning back to her work.

Chad and Kate looked at each other, and Chad shrugged. He guessed there was nothing to worry about, like Mom always said. But it would have been easier not to worry if it were his mother on the phone. She would have asked to speak to him.

Chad and Kate sat fidgeting while they watched for their mother out the window. Eventually, a police car stopped in the drive in front of the school entrance, and the uniformed cop glanced at them as he hurried in. What was going on? He bent to whisper to the receptionist, who immediately went and knocked on the principal's office door. She and the officer went in then and shut the door.

A minute later the principal and the receptionist came out. The receptionist went back to her desk without looking at the kids. The principal, a grandmotherly woman with white hair, came and bent down before Chad and Kate. "Would you join Officer Flanagan in my office, please?"

Chad wanted to ask what it was all about, but deep in his stomach he was afraid he knew. As he and Kate entered the principal's office, the principal stayed outside and shut the door. Officer Flanagan sat at a small table and pointed to two chairs. The kids sat down.

The officer was not smiling. "Chad and Kate, is it?" he said.

They nodded.

"Chad, I need to get some information from you. What time is your father expected to arrive?"

"In an hour. Why?"

"And you and your sister and your mom were going to meet him?"

"What happened to him?" Chad demanded.

"I'm afraid I have some bad news for you," Officer Flanagan said. "But it's not about your father."

CHAPTER 2

Dad's Announcement

I wish there was another way to tell you," Officer Flanagan told Chad and Kate, "and I wish I could wait until your dad was here with you. But there would be no keeping it from you. Your mother was in an accident on the way here. It wasn't her fault. The other driver ran a red light and hit her car broadside."

Chad noticed Kate trying to speak, but it seemed she couldn't make a sound. So Chad asked the question for both of them. "How bad was she hurt?"

"I'm sorry, kids...your mother was killed," Officer Flanagan said.

Kate's eyes grew wide and she began to shake and then cry. Chad wished he could cry. He wanted to reach over and hold Kate, but he couldn't move. This had to be a bad dream. He would wake up soon and start the day over. Yet, deep inside, he knew better.

Officer Flanagan put an arm around Kate's shoulder, keeping one eye on Chad. Chad didn't know what the officer expected him to do, but there was no need to worry. Chad felt himself growing cold. He couldn't even seem to move his eyes. He stared at the officer's face, but everything else seemed to turn dark.

His mind whirred. What would happen next? How would they tell Dad? What would they do without Mom? A happy day that couldn't be ruined by a seventh-grade bully had suddenly become the worst day of Chad's whole life.

Officer Flanagan opened the door and the principal returned, taking over with Kate. The policeman then asked Chad if there was a relative or a family friend he would like to have with them.

"No," Chad managed. "Our closest relatives are a couple of hours away, and I want to see my dad as soon as he gets off the plane."

"I can understand that. Anyone you'd like to have ride along with us? Your pastor? A teacher? A neighbor?"

Chad shook his head. He could probably think of someone if he tried. But he just wanted to get to his dad as soon as possible. "Are you going to take us?" Chad asked. "Because we'd better get going."

All the way to the airport, Chad and Kate huddled together in the back seat. Kate cried and cried, but different emotions welled up in Chad. He was angry. How could this have happened? Who ran a red light and killed his mom? He had worried about his dad getting back. Nothing had better happen to him! He was all they had left.

Usually when Chad was in trouble or bad things happened, he prayed. Now he couldn't pray. What would he say? "Take my mom to heaven"? He knew that was already answered. "Send her back"? That wasn't going to happen. "Where were You when this happened?" That sounded disrespectful, but it was what he was thinking.

How *could* God have let this happen? Chad knew that being a Christian didn't mean your life was perfect, but how did this fit in with the faith of their family? They had prayed for each other, that God would "bless Mom and Dad and Kate and Chad" for as long as he could remember. Didn't *bless* mean *protect*?

He didn't feel like much of a Christian right now, but it didn't seem like his fault. How was he supposed to feel? He was scared and he was mad. Worst of all, he knew this ugly news would stay with him forever. All he wanted now was to see his dad.

When they arrived at the small airport, about thirty miles north of Mukluk, Officer Flanagan took the kids into the waiting area. "Your dad's gonna see me and size this up pretty quick," he said. "I need you to give me a minute with him, okay? I need to make sure he hears it right, then you can have him all to yourselves."

As Chad and Kate sat in the molded plastic chairs, scanning the sky for the sight of their father's small plane, Chad felt a tightness in his chest that made him want to scream and shout. He wanted to break something, to throw something, to hit someone. But who would he hit? This sure wasn't Officer Flanagan's fault. Or Kate's. Or his dad's. He hated this feeling. The news was so terrible he didn't want to think about it, but he wondered if he would ever be able to think about anything else.

His dad would look for their welcoming smiles, but there would be none. If anything was worse than hearing that your mom was dead, it was thinking about how your dad would feel when he found out about it.

Kate was the first to spot the black speck in the cloudy sky. The day was already growing dark, though it was only mid-afternoon. They stood and watched as the small plane touched down and then taxied back to let off its only passenger. Bruce Michaels appeared on the steps of the small craft, stretching and running a hand through his sandy brown hair. He was stocky and muscular, and Chad noticed he had already changed out of his uniform into khaki pants and leather jacket.

Dad peered toward the little terminal, then helped the pilot un-load his bags from the underbelly of the plane. As they carried the stuff in, Bruce Michaels was clearly looking for three familiar faces. Chad and Kate hung back as Officer Flanagan stood by the door.

Dad's expectant smile faded as he saw the policeman. And when Officer Flanagan quickly told him what had happened, Dad staggered and had to sit down. He looked for the kids and they ran to him. Dad wept openly, and Kate sobbed again. Chad wanted to cry more than ever, but that anger, that heaviness inside him, wouldn't allow it. He buried his head in his dad's chest and held on as if he would never let go.

During the next several days, relatives and friends and people from the church filled the Michaels' house, and some stayed with Chad and Kate as Dad made the funeral arrangements.

It was nice to hear all the wonderful comments about his mother at the funeral, but Chad couldn't help wondering, *If she was so great, why didn't God leave her here?* It didn't help when he learned that the other driver in the accident had been drunk. And unhurt.

Many people said they had never seen a church come together so quickly over a tragedy. Kathryn Michaels had been a Sunday school teacher, and several kids said they had received Christ in her classes. One girl said she had been putting off her decision, but now realized that you never knew how much time you had to come to Christ.

"Maybe that one girl was the reason for what happened," Dad said, but Chad wondered why God couldn't have reached her without letting his mother die.

Dad and the other adults did a lot of praying over the next couple of weeks, but Chad couldn't even pray silently by himself. He didn't understand what had happened, and he didn't like it.

He didn't want to burden his father with his troubling thoughts, so every time Dad asked, "How ya doin', Spitfire?" Chad just nodded and tried to smile. Kids at school didn't know what to say, so they mostly said nothing. Nobody bugged Chad about dropping out of the daily snowball fight.

Kate started clinging to their dad as if she never wanted him out of her sight again. They worked on radios together and talked a lot.

Chad kept to himself and his computer. He could tell Dad was worried about him, and while he didn't like what was going on in his mind, he couldn't shake the anger. It was more than grief. He was mad, but didn't know who to be mad at. So he took it out on everyone.

As the school year wound down, Chad's grades dropped. He still did better than most of the kids in class, but he was no longer the top student. He was short-tempered and often sarcastic with his friends. He and Kate talked very little, because he knew if he said anything he might hassle her about being such a baby. But inside he felt like a baby, too.

Frequently now Chad found his dad on the phone talking business. Something was up, because whenever he came into the room, Dad changed the subject or quit talking.

Finally, one night about a month before the end of the school year, Dad called a family meeting. It was the first time they had had one without Mom. Chad and Kate sat down in front of the fireplace and waited for their dad to speak.

"You kids know I'm a plain guy," Dad began, stoking the fire.

"A plane guy or a plain guy?" Kate interrupted, giggling.

Dad smiled. "Plain, as in ordinary."

"I wouldn't call being a fighter pilot ordinary," Chad said.

"That's history, Spitfire," Bruce Michaels said. "Now I'm just a businessman with ten small planes, a crew of pilots, and too much work to do. At least I was."

"I wish *I* had a nickname," Kate interrupted.

"I could call you Sparky," Dad said. "That's what they call the radio techies in the military. But *Kate* is already a nickname. You were named after your mom, but a nickname never seemed to fit her. I always called her Kathryn."

The three of them sat in silence for a moment, the only sound the crackling of the fire. It was hard to think about Mom.

Finally, Chad broke the silence. "What do you mean, 'At least I *was*'? You're not still Mr. Yukon Do It Man?"

Dad shook his head. "You know that since we lost Mom I have quit flying so I can be here before and after school. But still I have all the other pilots and flights to worry about."

"I know," Kate said. "Seems like you're always busy."

"Well, that's changed now." He went on to explain that he had sold his business, planes, cargo, routes, and even the contracts with his pilots.

Chad was stunned. He had never thought of his dad as anything but a pilot. "You're not going to fly anymore?" he said.

"I'll always fly," Dad said. "Don't worry about that. But I had to get in a position where I don't have to be away. This sale gives me that freedom."

"So, are we rich?" Chad blurted.

"There you go, Spitfire," Dad said. "Jumping the gun as

usual. The truth is, we've never been poor. You know there's never anything you really want or need that we can't afford."

"Then why do we have to chip in on everything?" Kate said. "You always make us pay half out of our allowance if it's anything big or special."

"True," Dad said. "Because that's how life is. Anything worth having, like all your electronics stuff, is worth working for. Nobody will ever just give you things. You'll be glad we raised you that way. Growing up, my family never seemed to have enough. We had to work for everything."

Chad was still reeling from the news that his dad no longer owned the charter flight business, but he didn't know how to say it. "So are we rich now or not?" he insisted.

"Let me put it this way," Dad said. "I was taught that if you work hard, treat people right, and, as the Bible says, 'do everything heartily as unto the Lord,' you'll be all right."

Chad couldn't sit still. He moved closer to the fire and watched the light from the flames shining on his dad's cheek. He couldn't contain his sarcasm any longer. "Yeah, you do all that stuff and then your wife gets killed. You call that being all right?"

"Chad!" Kate scolded.

"It's okay, Kate," Dad said. "I've had my questions about all this too. I don't understand why your mom had to die either. But if that one girl became a Christian because of it, you know your mom would have—"

"I know," Chad said quickly. "I don't want to hear that again, okay? Are you going to tell us whether we're rich now, or not?"

Chad was surprised his dad didn't simply send him to his room for talking like that. Dad hesitated, then answered him.

"Yes, we are," he said. "I want to tell you both this, because it's important. It's an answer to prayer, but it comes with tremendous responsibility."

Dad was talking like Dad always talked. Everything was a big deal, everything was serious. But Chad was beginning to think that maybe this was for real, maybe this really was serious.

"I'd been praying about changing my life so that by the end of the school year I could spend more time at home," Dad continued. "I didn't know it would mean selling my business, but that's what it came to."

"But you love your business!" Kate said.

"I love flying, and I'll still do that. It won't be hard to give up the rest of it. But this is the important part. I sold the business for much more than I ever dreamed I would."

"How much?" Chad said.

"I'm not going to tell you, Spitfire," Dad said, "because you wouldn't understand it much more than I do. Let's just say it's almost a hundred times more than I ever expected to see in my life."

"Wow," Kate said. Chad whistled.

"Of course there are huge taxes to pay, but I wouldn't be able to spend the rest in two lifetimes. I would never have to work again. But that's not how I was made. I feel a tremendous responsibility to use this money the way God would want us to. So we're going to give half of it to God's work."

There's that "tremendous responsibility" thing again, Chad thought.

"I want you two to pray about forming a new company that would be made up of just the three of us. I want to use my flying skills and this extra money to help with the work of God around the world. Would you do that?"

Kate was excited, but Chad just shrugged. He didn't want to

hurt his dad, but he wondered why he would want to give so much to God—money and time and everything—when God had let his wife die.

Over the next few weeks, Kate and Dad talked about it every chance they got. They dreamed of flying all over the globe as a family, helping missionaries wherever they could.

Chad just listened and tried not to be sarcastic. When Dad wasn't around, Kate tried to find out why Chad wasn't excited. "Think of what we can do and where we can go!" she said.

"I don't want to go anywhere," he answered. "Who wants to go halfway around the world? Who knows what kind of food they would have or whether they even have running water?"

But finally it became official. The little family of Spitfire, Kate, and Bruce Michaels would become the Global Air Troubleshooters. Dad would let missionary groups know that he was available for anything they needed.

He could build planes, fix planes, fly planes, fill in for someone who was home on furlough, whatever they needed. He could even repair radios, with Kate's help. He would go only when Chad and Kate could join him, because he never wanted to be separated from the family again. Most of their missions would be over the summer, but if Dad were needed somewhere else during the school year, he would even take the kids out of school and either hire a tutor or teach them himself.

Then one day Dad announced that immediately after school was out for the summer, the family would leave for Indonesia. Inter-Indonesian Mission had asked Dad to evaluate their small fleet of single and twin-engine planes and recommend whether they needed new ones. He would also fill in as a pilot as needed.

Chad would rather have done anything but go to Indonesia.

CHAPTER 3

The Trip

O ne evening, about a week before the family was to leave for Indonesia, Dad knocked at Chad's bedroom door.

"I'm on-line," Chad said as his dad quietly entered and sat down.

"I'll wait," Dad said.

"I'm just writing to Uncle Bill in Portland."

"About?"

"You know."

"Chad, I don't want you to stay with Uncle Bill after all. You're going with Kate and me."

Chad quickly saved his work, exited the system, and shut down his computer. "Why?"

"Because the whole point of our new company is being together. I know you miss your mom. So does Kate and so do I. That's why I want us together. You kids are growing up fast and you'll leave home some day. I want as much time with you as I can get."

Chad didn't know how to answer that. He hadn't been acting like anyone his dad would want to spend more time with. "Dad, you know I'm not into all that outdoor rough stuff. Indonesia, especially where we're going, is full of jungles. And I'll bet they're not even on the Internet."

"Well, maybe you can help get them up to speed."

"Dad, I don't want to go, and I don't know why I have to."

"I don't want to have to make you go, Chad. But neither Kate nor I would want to go without you."

"Kate wouldn't care."

"If you believe that, you don't really know Kate. She loves you. And you love her too, even if you've gotten out of the habit of telling her."

Chad stared at the dark computer screen. Of course he loved Kate, but not enough to want to go to Indonesia with her. "So you're making me go."

"Like I said, I don't want to have to do that."

"But I don't have any choice?"

"When you put it that way, no."

Chad shook his head.

"And I'd like you to have a good attitude about it."

"You want me to fake it, you mean?"

"I want you to not make the trip miserable for your sister and me with your negative attitude. You don't have to like it, but we don't want to hear about it all the time, okay?"

Chad sensed his father's anger.

"Okay?" his dad pressed.

"I'll try," he said.

"I also want you to be fair and open-minded. You might like this new experience. It's an unusual opportunity that few kids your age ever have. You'll learn a lot, and you might just become more of the outdoorsman you want to be."

"Who says I want to be that?"

"You complain about it all the time."

"That doesn't mean I want to be a nature-loving guy."

"Yes it does," Dad said.

Chad didn't respond. He hated it when his dad was right.

They flew from the airstrip north of Mukluk to Anchorage in Dad's own plane, then to Los Angeles by jet. From there they flew to a series of South Pacific Islands, through Sydney, Australia, and on to Jakarta, capital of the huge island of Indonesia.

After a few days of getting used to the sticky heat and the new time zone, they flew more than two thousand miles to Sentani, near the Irian Jaya-Papua New Guinea border. They stayed at the Inter-Indonesian Mission compound near Sentani. And until they headed back to Alaska, all their flights would be on tiny single- and twin-engine planes.

So far Chad had hated every minute of it. The heat, the humidity, the bugs, the inconvenience—everything made him wish he was home, or at least with his Uncle Bill in Oregon. As exhausting and strange as the trip had been, Kate seemed to love getting to know the missionaries and their families. She got to learn about radios she had never seen before. Chad kept his distance, but he had to admit that he enjoyed seeing his dad happy again.

Dad spent the first ten days mostly in the Inter-Indonesian Mission hangar at the Sentani airstrip. Kate flew several test flights with him, and Chad watched him get greasy from head to toe, tearing engines apart and putting them back together again. Dad recommended to IIM that they upgrade the technology on several of their planes, and when they balked at the cost, he insisted on ordering the parts and paying for them himself.

Chad kept begging his way out of the flights into the jungle. He stayed at the mission compound and was allowed to play with one of the computers. He wouldn't admit he was a little jealous when Kate came back with stories about the tribespeople of that area and their strange clothes and food and huts, but still Chad wanted no part of the jungle.

They had a long flight planned in a few days, and Chad knew his dad wanted him to go along. So he began trying to think of reasons why he should stay in Sentani. "I'm really getting to learn the computer setup here," he told his dad. "It's outdated, but it's interesting."

The next day, however, Chad got himself into trouble, and there was no way his dad would let him out of going on the flight. Chad had searched the entire system on the computer and discovered an internal modem, an old, slow one. He pored over the manuals and used everything he had ever learned about computers, and somehow he got the thing plugged into the phone system and hooked up to the international Internet. Before long he had transmitted a letter to his Uncle Bill, pleading with him to call and talk sense into Dad, urging him to let Chad come home.

The only problem was, the system was so old, the modem so slow, and the phone system in Indonesia so limited that the transmission took more than two hours. Chad's letter never reached his uncle, but by the end of the day, the mission received a call from the local phone company informing them that the computer transmission had cost hundreds of dollars.

The transmission was, of course, easily traced to Chad. That night was not a fun one. He received the lecture of his life.

"Of course I'll reimburse the mission," Dad said. "And you will reimburse me."

"That'll take me forever!" Chad said.

"You may have to do some extra work when we get home," Dad said.

"You ought to pay me for being here," Chad muttered.

"Chad," Dad said, sighing, "you act like this is someone else's fault. You did this and you have to live with the consequences. And one of those is that you're going with Kate and me tomorrow when we take Dr. Howlett to Yawsikor."

"Who's that?"

"You met him. Dr. George Howlett is the Inter-Indonesian Mission president. He's making a delivery to missionaries working with a pre-Stone Age tribal group in the jungle near Bime (Bee´ may). Then we take him on to Yawsikor on the other side of the island, about 250 miles from here. He's going to a missions conference there, and then he'll be flown on to Jakarta for a flight to the United States."

"Can I go with him?" asked Chad, only half kidding.

"Not on your life. Now get some sleep. We leave before dawn."

"Before dawn!?"

"Of course. The flight curfews are late morning here because of the winds. We have to fly to Bime, then to Yawsikor and all the way back here, all in the morning."

"Oh, brother."

"And I don't want any attitude, you hear?"

Chad pursed his lips and nodded. He knew he had no one to blame but himself.

At five-thirty the next morning, Dr. Howlett loaded his luggage onto the twin-engine plane, carefully weighing it first. "I've got lots of goodies for the kids in Bime and Yawsikor," he said. "They always expect it. And see this cooler? You could drop this from the plane and it wouldn't break open. I'm taking some food from a Chinese restaurant in Jayapura for the missionaries."

Chad secretly liked Dr. Howlett, because he didn't seem like a typical executive. He dressed like a normal person with a light pullover shirt and shorts, and usually tennis shoes, though today he wore tall hiking boots. He was a robust man who had himself flown these rugged jungle areas for years.

When they boarded the tiny twin-engine four-seater, Dr. Howlett helped the kids into the rear seats, Chad behind his dad and Kate next to Chad. Then Dr. Howlett climbed in next to Mr. Michaels to help with the preflight checklist. Dad stretched the microphone cord back so Kate could lean forward and reach it. As they taxied onto the runway, she spoke, "Kilo double Hotel forty-forty-eight to tower."

"Tower, go ahead."

"Preflight finished, ready for takeoff to Bime, continuing to Yawsikor."

"You're clear, forty-forty-eight. Blue skies. Bime and Yawsikor wind curfews are nine-thirty this morning. Ours is ten-thirty, so hurry back."

"Roger, tower."

And they were off.

Dr. Howlett turned, straining against his seat belt to talk with Chad and Kate. He had to shout over the engine noise: "Our first stop is right in the middle of a huge 1976 earthquake area," he said. "I remember flying over it a few years after the earthquake, and still seeing where the vegetation had been stripped from the sides of the mountains, and rivers had been dammed up. To look at it today, you'd never know there had been one of the biggest earthquakes ever in this region."

Dr. Howlett peeked at Bruce Michaels' flight map. "We won't be able to stay long at Bime, but the next leg of the flight will take us over the mountains. You'll be able to see Mt. Juliana, which is about fifteen thousand feet high. Just over the other side you'll see an area we call Cannibal Valley. The small Braza tribe there is cannibalistic, and we have been unable to get to them since the earthquake."

Kate leaned forward, straining to hear. "I thought you said that was more than twenty years ago!" she shouted.

"It was, but the quake closed off the way to them by river. It actually caused the Braza River to change course, and now there's no way to get to the Brazas unless they would allow us to land a helicopter there. And they won't."

"And they eat people?" Chad asked.

Dr. Howlett nodded. "They used to," he said. "There have been no reports of cannibalism in these jungles for many years, but without any recent contact with the Brazas, we just don't know."

"Don't they need water?" Chad's dad asked.

"The change of the river's course produced a sort of fresh-water lake for them, but they're pretty much limited to a small area now. They would have to walk a long way to put a craft on the river and travel anywhere. We think it has kept them from warring with other tribes, but it has also kept them from hearing the Gospel."

During the flight to Bime, Chad's dad explained how he always kept an emergency landing spot in sight between airstrips.

"They are just openings, clearings. You'd never choose to put down there, but if you have to, you have to. I find a spot and keep my eye on it until I can't see it anymore. I figure if I can see it, I can reach it if we have engine failure. Back home there are all kinds of places to land in an emergency, but here where there are no roads and very few landing strips, you have to keep track of your spots."

"All our pilots do this," Dr. Howlett said. "They spend almost their entire time looking for the next clearing."

The flight was smooth and the landing on the tiny airstrip at Bime was bumpy but exciting. Bruce Michaels landed the twin-engine plane uphill, and parked at the high end of the runway, not far from one of the mission houses. Dr. Howlett explained it was necessary to land uphill. "That slows the plane and allows you a shorter runway. When we take off again, we'll start downhill to get up enough speed to get airborne."

"But there's a mountain at the end of the runway going that way," Chad said.

"So there is!" Dr. Howlett smiled. "And it rises to fifteen thousand feet, so when we take off again, your dad will have to fly in circles until he's high enough to get over it."

The plane was quickly surrounded by missionary families and tribal people. Chad felt as if he and Kate were in a movie or a dream. He had seen pictures of people like this, but he had never expected to see them close up.

They were barefoot, wore hardly any clothes, and some wore bones through their noses. Dr. Howlett explained that they lived nearby in a village of thatched-roof huts, and the missionaries were learning their language and telling them about Christ. "That's what I did with the Brazas, more than twenty-five years ago."

"*You* worked with the Brazas?" Chad asked.

"I wasn't the only one," Dr. Howlett said. "Mr. Coleman, who runs this mission station right here, and I went the long way around and arrived by canoe. We made contact with just a few of them. After several secret visits they warned us we were in danger from some of their violent tribespeople, and so were they, if they saw us again. We had learned just enough of their language to present a simple Gospel. One man they called Jonga tried to say my name. He called me George-George and Mr. Coleman Man-Man."

Dr. Howlett and the Global Air Troubleshooters were on the ground in Bime for less than half an hour. Kate looked over the little ground radio setup and made a quick friend of one of the missionary children. Dad helped Dr. Howlett unload two boxes of supplies, then went looking for Kate and her new friend. Chad explored the mission house.

The elderly couple who lived there, the Colemans, had served in Bime now for more than thirty years. Mrs. Coleman told Chad that their own children had grown up there and were now involved in their own ministries. "You'll have to run along now," she said, "because we have an important meeting with Dr. Howlett, and then you will have to be on your way."

Dr. Howlett went into the mission house with a grim-faced national of about twenty years old who came from the nearby village. Chad was curious, so he tiptoed onto the makeshift porch of the stilted frame home and sat with his back to the screenless window, listening. He knew this was none of his business, but he never got to listen in on adult conversations. He hadn't asked to be in this wild country anyway. If he couldn't be at a computer, at least he could sit there and listen.

CHAPTER 4

Cannibal Valley

D r. Howlett had been called in to help make peace between the Colemans and their houseboy, Waman. Since Dr. Howlett didn't speak Waman's dialect, they all spoke in Pidgin, which almost anyone can understand if they listen closely. From what Chad could make out, the Colemans suspected the boy of teaching children from his village that the Christians were liars, and that the superstitious beliefs of the tribe made up the only true religion.

Mrs. Coleman had confronted Waman and he had denied it, but she had heard from others she trusted in the nearby village that much in Waman's life was not as it appeared when he showed up at the weekly church service. "What breaks my heart," she said, "is that we love him. We led him to the Lord. We know he understands the truth."

Dr. Howlett sounded very grave as he spoke to Waman. "We simply cannot tolerate your deceit. If you choose your own religion over the truth of the Bible, that is your choice. But to pretend to be a believer and then to war against Christ and the church, that is even worse. The Colemans love you and know that you know better. They do not believe your denials. I would have hoped you and they could come to some agreement. But I choose to believe them, and as they have asked me to become involved, I must tell you my decision. You will not be allowed to work for them as long as you are an enemy of God. You must stay in your own village and not come to the mission compound. If you wish to confess, however, the Colemans will forgive you and welcome you back."

Chad turned and peeked through the window. The Colemans were crying and nodding at the houseboy. But Waman looked angry. He began to shout in his own dialect, and Chad couldn't understand him.

"Yes," Mr. Coleman responded in Pidgin, "there is a young woman from your village who works here and who is not yet a believer. But she doesn't claim to be one and then live another way. You once claimed to be a Christian."

Waman stood and argued again. It sounded to Chad as if he were saying that he rejected the accusations as well as Dr. Howlett's authority. He no longer wanted to work for people who would think such things of him.

Dr. Howlett spoke softly to the Colemans. "I must ask you once again, are you certain that you are right to suspect him?"

They both nodded sadly.

"Then your offer of forgiveness stands and you must regretfully accept his decision."

With that, Waman ran from the house, yelling.

"He curses us," the woman said. "It's so sad. We have always loved him, and we thought he understood the Gospel.

"We'll pray God speaks to his conscience and that he returns," Dr. Howlett said.

Chad was startled when Waman flew past him. He wanted to follow the young man, but he was afraid the Colemans and Dr. Howlett might see him on that side of the house and know he had been listening. So he scampered around the other way and found his dad and Kate saying good-bye to her new friend.

They headed back around to the other side of the mission house and boarded the little plane for the next leg of the flight. Dr. Howlett appeared and talked about the compassion of the Colemans.

"That's why we're here," he said. "When I see how devoted these missionaries are to getting the good news to these tribes, I want to do anything I can for them. I miss being on the front lines myself."

While the little plane struggled to gain altitude, Kate was obviously working hard to hear, but the big man couldn't turn any further in his seat.

"How about I trade places with you, Chad?" Dr. Howlett said. "I want to tell you more about when I worked with the Brazas years ago."

Chad had wanted to sit next to his dad anyway, so he quickly agreed. While Dr. Howlett carefully climbed into the back, Chad clambered over him to the front, next to his dad, and strapped himself in. It was easier for him to turn and listen, and now both he and Kate could hear Dr. Howlett. The older man then told them how he had learned to greet Jonga and a few other Brazas and to tell them he had come in peace.

"We used the wordless book, a book with a green cover and four inside pages, all blank and in four colors—black, red, white, and gold. With the black page I tried to show them that, like all of us, their hearts were dark with sin. The red page showed that God's son Jesus shed His blood and died for them, paying the penalty for their sin. That brought them to the white page, which showed that their hearts could be white as snow. The gold page represented heaven. I walked them through those pages several times. I even left a few copies of the wordless book."

"What is the green cover for?" Kate asked.

Dr. Howlett got a faraway look in his eyes. "Green signifies growth, the way Christians are supposed to grow in Christ. I simply wasn't there long enough to know whether they understood and became believers, let alone whether they grew at all. The last time we tried to land a helicopter there, the Brazas shook their fists and waved weapons at us."

"What did their language sound like?" Kate asked.

"*Treetzee* is a Braza word that means warm, sunshine, peace, friendly—all those things at once."

"It sounds like an ice cream cone," Kate said, and they all laughed.

"*Shaka* means hello. And the word *benboon* means gift or present."

Kate began saying "Shaka, treetzee, benboon," over and over to Chad, to her dad, and even to Dr. Howlett, who repeated the same back to her. "Do you have a benboon for me?" she asked, laughing. "Those cannibals wouldn't have any idea what I was saying, besides *benboon*, would they?"

Dr. Howlett smiled at Chad and Kate as they made up other words and pretended to converse in Braza dialect. Then he grew quiet, yawned, and stretched his legs into the tiny opening between Chad's and his dad's front seats. "Hey, you kids can start looking for Cannibal Valley pretty soon," he said. "Let me know if you see any of the nationals—people who are native inhabitants of this country—or any smoke from cooking fires down there."

He folded his arms then, lay his head to one side, and soon fell asleep.

Dad turned a crank under the instrument panel several times.

"What're you doing?" Chad asked.

"Letting out the radio antenna wire."

"What's that?"

"Fifty feet of wire that extends out the back of the plane."

"What's it for?" Chad asked.

"Tell him, Kate."

"The radio antenna wire makes the plane a bigger target for radio signals," she said, "especially when you're flying in the mountains. You reel it out when you're up and reel it back in before you land."

As Dad set their course for Yawsikor, Chad grew tired of looking for Cannibal Valley. It all looked the same to him. There was a valley all right, as far as the eye could see. The entire side of the mountain range was overgrown, and he saw nothing of anyone or anything else. He tried to see where the river had changed course, but he had no idea what that would look like, so he didn't know what to look for.

In fact, there were no clearings anywhere. What would they use in case of an emergency? Chad wondered if his dad had his eye on any spots. He glanced over, but his dad was no longer scanning the horizon.

Dad had clearly quit looking for places to land. He seemed more concerned with the instrument panel, especially the fuel gauge. He tapped it, then rapped hard on it. Chad leaned over to take a peek.

"Does that say what I think it says?"

"It has to be a mistake," Dad said. "I fueled this plane myself. It has to be a gauge problem."

"Shouldn't you be looking for clearings?" Chad said. "Like before?"

Dad ignored him, so Chad looked for clearings himself. Still, he saw nothing but trees and jungle. Except for a few muddy rivers, nothing lay below them but green, green, and more green. Even the mountainsides of the Great Dividing Range were covered with foliage.

Despite all the flights he'd been on with his dad, Chad had never before been on a plane that was in trouble. He stole a glance at Kate in the seat behind him. Had she noticed that Dad had changed his routine, that he was tapping hard on the fuel gauge? But Kate was idly drinking from a bottle of distilled water and looking out the window, obviously trying to get a glimpse of Cannibal Valley.

Up to this point, Chad had almost been glad he had come on this flight. But now something was wrong. He didn't want to worry Kate, and Dr. Howlett was still asleep.

"Dad," Chad said. "Are we all right?"

Dad held up a hand. "Chad, please!"

"Is there anything I can do?"

"I don't know yet. I just hope this is an instrument problem."

Dad, now studying the horizon again, got on the radio. "Bime radio, come in please. Kilo double Hotel forty-forty-eight to Bime radio."

Dad repeated his call several times. Chad knew that the radio at small stations like that was usually on only a few hours a day, but wouldn't someone monitor it for at least a little while after a takeoff?

Dad tried his transmission again, and finally the voice of Mrs. Coleman came on.

"This is Bime radio, go ahead."

"Roger, Bime. We just took off from there and I've got a low fuel reading."

"Did you fuel at Sentani?" she asked.

"Roger."

"Then you should be good to Yawsikor. You think it's an instrument problem?"

"Hoping."

"Roger. You want to be safe and set back down here?"

"Negative, but I don't see any clearings here, either. We're across the divide, pointed at Yawsikor. Is there any place on this side I could get down if I had to?"

"Roger, you should see some clearings in about fifteen minutes."

"Roger."

"We'll be praying for you."

"Thanks!" Dad replaced the mike.

"She doesn't sound very concerned," Chad said.

"I'm sure this is everyday stuff for them," Dad said. "We'd better both be right about the gauge, though. It says we have no fuel left, let alone fifteen-minutes' worth. We couldn't even get back to Bime if we ran out now. We couldn't climb back over the divide. But there is a small reserve fuel tank. I just have to switch over to it."

"Good!"

"Maybe not so good. The first tank shouldn't even be close to empty, and both tanks feed the engine from the same line. If the problem is in the line, we may have plenty of fuel and no way to get it to the engines."

He reached under the instrument panel. "The reserve tank switch handle is right under here. Ah..." He smiled at Chad. "It's a loose wire running from the fuel gauge. I was worried for nothing, as usual."

Chad breathed a heavy sigh of relief. "Hope I didn't do that," he said.

"It was probably our passenger," his dad answered. "When you two switched places, he must have caught it with his foot. I might even have done it when I was letting out the antenna wire."

Chad nodded and began looking for clearings again, just in case.

"I see a valley, but I don't see any cannibals," Kate grumbled behind him.

And then the engines began to cough and sputter. Within seconds both had died, and his dad was maneuvering the controls as if playing a huge musical instrument. Chad watched as he quickly switched to the reserve fuel tank and frantically tried to restart the engine. Loose wire or not, faulty gauge or not, enough fuel or not, the plane had no power. They were going down!

"Dad!" Chad shouted.

"Quiet!" his dad said, and quiet it was. The racket of the noisy engines had stopped, and now they heard only the dead stillness of gliding at high altitude. But Chad could hear his heart slamming in his chest.

"Why did you turn it off, Dad?" Kate said, leaning forward.

No one answered.

"Should we wake up Dr. Howlett?" Chad asked.

Dad shook his head. "Nothing he can do," he said. "And we won't glide long. I'll use the flaps to level us. I just don't want to hit nose first."

"Can't you restart it?"

"I'm trying!"

He manipulated the controls, but Chad could feel the momentum change from forward to downward. Kate began to cry, and Chad wanted to.

"What can we do?" Chad said.

"Pray!"

"I already am!"

"Me too!" Kate said.

The nose of the plane turned down even more, and Chad felt the pressure build in his ears as they descended. He knew his dad was doing everything he could to keep the plane level, but what good would that do if they had nowhere to land?

"If we hit the ground," Dad said tersely, "let's hope those fuel tanks are empty. If the engines don't restart, the best I can do is skim the trees and hope for a clearing. If we're shut off when we hit, we're going straight down."

"Will that kill us?" Kate asked.

"I don't know," Dad said.

"Will we wake up in heaven with Mom?"

"I believe it!"

"So do I," Chad said, "but I'm scared."

"So am I," Dad answered. "Is there any room in the back? We need as much weight back there as possible!"

Chad looked back to where Dr. Howlett had stored his cargo. They had unloaded only a couple of boxes at Bime. "Kate and I might be able to fit back there. You want us to try?"

"You'd better. Now hurry!"

"Will that save us?" Kate asked.

"I don't know," Dad said. "But we have to try!"

Chad and Kate scrambled past the sleeping Dr. Howlett and climbed in among the cargo. Chad felt his stomach rise as the plane shuddered and shook against the wind resistance. The cargo shifted forward and pushed at the restraints. Chad and Kate held on to keep from tumbling to the front of the plane. Dr. Howlett seemed suspended forward, held by only his seat belt. That woke him.

He clutched the back of Dad's seat. "What's happening?" he said. "Throttle up!"

"No power!" Dad said. "We lost our fuel somehow!"

Dad adjusted the flaps to fight the wind. The plane went from a steep dive to another long glide, which made Chad feel better for only an instant. They were still about to crash, that was certain. He only hoped that somehow they could survive.

But Dr. Howlett grabbed his Bible from his briefcase on the floor and held it tight to his chest. "Lord," he said, "spare us with a miracle or take us all at once. Don't leave one of us alone in a place like this!"

CHAPTER 5

The Crash

One more sweep away from the mountain and we're going down!" Dad shouted. "Hang on!"

Chad had never been so scared in his life as they plunged toward the earth faster than any roller coaster he had ever ridden.

Dr. Howlett reached back with his long right arm and pressed his hand against one of his cargo boxes, just under where Chad and Kate lay. "You kids get as far back in the plane as you can!" he shouted.

The plane seemed vertical now, nose pointed almost straight down. Every time Chad's dad adjusted the flaps, the cargo slid away from the tail a foot or so, and Chad and Kate hooked their toes on the edges and pushed hard with their hands to keep from dropping to the front of the plane. Chad could see Dr. Howlett straining to keep the cargo from crushing him, one hand jammed against it and the other clutching the back of Dad's seat. His face was red and covered with sweat, as if he knew he would be sandwiched between the ground and the cargo if they hit.

Chad caught sight of the flaps on the tiny wings struggling to level the plane one more time. Metal and plastic squeaked and groaned as the free-falling craft picked up speed. When the blue outside turned to green, Chad waited for certain death. He and Kate embraced each other, and they heard Dad yell, "I love you kids!"

Chad turned to look at Kate. Her face was a mask of terror. It appeared she wanted to say something, but no words came. They hung onto each other, and as the plane made its last desperate swoop from vertical to almost horizontal, Chad felt the pressure on his body give way. There was now a foot and a half or so of space between the cargo and the tiny rear of the plane.

He pulled with his toes and yanked Kate with him. As they heard first leaves and then branches batter the bottom of the plane, they tumbled into the crevice in the back. Huddled there, their bodies and heads jammed together as if they were one person with eight limbs, Chad heard Kate moan as the plane blasted into the tops of trees.

For the briefest instant, in spite of the noise, it seemed as if the treetops had violently slowed the plane and that it was level. But then they were spinning. From the racket and the direction of the lurch, Chad knew a wing had caught a branch or the trunk of a tree. They were whirled in a circle so fast that Chad almost lost consciousness.

Something ripped a hole in the tail of the plane, and Chad glimpsed the wing that had just been sheered off teetering in a treetop and then cartwheeling to the ground. Kate seemed unconscious already, and Chad wished he were. He didn't want to feel whatever it was that might finally knock him out.

Leaves and branches and vines banged the hurtling plane and made a deafening roar. Chad shut his eyes tight as the plane spun and bounced end over end. The remaining wing bashed into something and the plane seemed to stop dead in the trees, all the weight shifting forward. If they hit the ground, Chad's dad and Dr. Howlett would surely be crushed by the heavy, shifting cargo.

With Kate limp by his side, Chad watched the cargo break through the restraints and smash into the two back seats, ripping them from their bolts in the floor and slamming them into the backs of the front seats. A great groan came from Dr. Howlett.

Chad and Kate slid over the top of the seats and hurtled toward their father who was trying to protect his head and face with his forearms as the side of the mountain and the jungle floor rushed to fill the windshield.

There seemed no space between the cargo and the cockpit now, and no sign of Dr. Howlett. But just before the plane crashed to the ground, it was jerked in yet another direction and bounced crazily on its side.

Barely conscious and hanging on for dear life, Chad could see out the front where the glass had blown out. The plane was hanging from some fibrous, viny tree only a few feet off the ground.

For an instant there was complete silence. Chad was aware of the heat, the humidity, the lack of any wind or even the slightest breeze to move the leaves, some sticking crazily through the holes ripped in the side of the plane. He heard liquid splashing. That had to be fuel, but from where? Would they now explode and burn?

With a squeal and a squeak, what was left of the plane dropped onto its right side, pulling free from the foliage and landing on what felt like solid rock. They had hit the side of the mountain two hundred feet from the valley floor, and they began to slide.

For a few seconds, nothing blocked their path. Chad's body was pasted against the side of the plane scraping down the mountain, and he fought to move away from the quickly heating sheet of metal.

"Kate?" he called out, as the sliding mass of twisted steel picked up speed again. No answer. And he couldn't see her.

"Dad?"

Nothing.

He didn't call out to Dr. Howlett. His body had to have been crushed between the cargo and Dad's seat from the first great weight shift.

When would this end? The plane kept skidding, sliding through the underbrush, scraping the side of the mountain. It hit something and spun, then dropped another twenty feet or so, blowing open another hole and dumping out cargo and Dr. Howlett.

Where was Kate? Had she already been thrown clear? And Dad! What would he find if he survived this last plunge? When would it stop?

The next several seconds seemed like minutes on a crazy carnival ride. Something made the careening carcass of what used to be the twin-engine plane spin halfway around again. Now they were dropping backward, tail first, down a ravine. By the time the wreckage finally came to a stop at the bottom of the mountainside, all that was left inside the mangled fuselage were Chad's father, the two front seats, the instrument panel, and Chad, his hand gripping mightily on a dangling bungi cord that had once corralled the cargo.

Again Chad was stunned by the utter lack of noise. He heard absolutely nothing. His ears still rang from the racket of brushing tree tops, banging, crashing, hanging, sliding, bumping, cargo-sliding, and finally slamming to a stop. Chad let out a huge breath and realized he had been holding it in since the last time he had called out for his dad. His stomach and chest heaved with the effort of catching his breath, and he felt the sobs well within him.

He couldn't imagine that anyone else had survived. He was sure Dr. Howlett's last prayer had been answered, and the answer was no. Had God left Chad alone in this horrible place? And why him? He suddenly realized that if he'd stayed in his original seat, he'd be where Dr. Howlett was right now. Where *was* Dr. Howlett? Where was Kate? And Dad?

Everything in him screamed at him to move forward, to pick past the debris and find Dad. What would he find? He didn't want to think about it.

Move! Move! Chad kept telling himself. But his fingers seemed paralyzed, forced into a fist around the wire and plastic and rubber bungi cord. He was crouched, almost as if he had surfed down that mountainside. He tried to straighten up, but his knees were swollen and sore and there wasn't room to stand inside the fuselage.

Chad reached with his free hand and pried his fingers from the cord. He tried to move again and his legs gave way. He slumped and sat, his back against the crumpled side of the plane. He had just enough room to straighten out his legs in front of him, and then he noticed he had lost both his shoes.

It seemed such a weird scene. Was this some kind of crazy nightmare? Would he wake up, and where? Would it be at home in Mukluk?

Or had he and his dad and sister really flown halfway around the world to Indonesia? Would he awaken in the mission home in Jakarta? Or at the compound near Sentani?

Though his mind was reeling, down deep Chad knew the truth. This was no dream. Sweat poured from him, and he felt a chill in spite of the overwhelming heat and humidity. As he stared at his puffy ankles, he wondered if all his joints were sprained. He moved his toes in circles and clenched and unclenched his fists, then reached out with both arms.

Finally, the numbness left, but he almost wished it hadn't. He didn't think he had any broken bones, but he was suddenly sore all over.

As Chad sat staring at his feet, not moving, a great fatigue washed over him. His heart still pounded and his breath came in great gasps. He was still terrified, especially as he thought about where he was and that he was alone. But something made him want to sleep, to roll onto his side, curl up, and close his eyes.

He could not. He would not. This was some strange physical reaction, maybe what they called shock. He didn't know. As he fought the urge to drift from consciousness, his hands began to shake. Soon his legs quivered, too. Then his whole body convulsed into shudders he could not control. Was this it? Would he be found, along with his dad and his sister and Dr. Howlett, by cannibals?

This uncontrollable shivering scared him. Did he really want to sleep? Did he want to die? If he lived, where would he go for help? Dr. Howlett had said this mountain was 15,000 feet high. How long would it take him to climb through the underbrush all the way up and then all the way down again to the mission station at Bime? He knew there was enough foliage to hang onto to get to the top, but even if he could evade the Brazas, could he get down the other side without falling? More important, could he stand or walk at all?

From where he sat, Chad could see the top of his dad's head. He wasn't sure he wanted to see more than that. Between the bowed front seats were the radio headphones, seemingly the only undamaged things in the plane.

Chad crossed his arms and stretched his legs, laying one painful ankle over the other. He fought to stop shivering, then rolled to his side and drew his knees to his chest. Overcome by hopelessness, he tucked his chin to his knees and the sobs came. Chad heard himself wailing in the otherwise eerie silence of the jungle wilderness, and he realized he had not cried since before his mother died.

Just minutes before, the flight had been perfect. As much as he had fought coming to Indonesia, he had started to change his mind about this trip. But now, because of, what?—some stupid glitch in the fuel line—everything had changed.

Kate was gone. Dr. Howlett was gone. Dad was not making a sound. The plane was a wreck. And Chad hardly recognized his own body.

Almost without thinking, Chad realized he was praying. He wasn't even saying anything specific. He was just calling out to God, "Please, help me." He didn't expect things to suddenly return to what they were just minutes before. He knew he wouldn't be given some kind of super power. He wasn't even hoping for that. All he wanted was help. And there was no one anywhere to give it to him. Except God.

Suddenly, Chad was no longer crying. He still shook, but he felt a resolve to stop. Somehow he knew that even though he couldn't do much, he might be the only one left who could do anything.

He sat up and clenched his fists painfully. No more crying, he told himself. No more sleeping or wishing he had not survived. He wanted to do what his dad would do, what his mom would be proud of, what his sister needed.

Chad struggled to all fours, his knees tender as he crawled out of the wreckage. Then, just before he was able to drop a couple of feet to the ground, he caught his shirt on a metal shard that hung him up for an instant before tearing loose. That caused him to fall on his hands and knees, and he might have laughed under different circumstances, and if it hadn't made him so mad. What more could go wrong? He could hardly walk, hardly move, and he couldn't even jump two feet.

He looked up the mountainside at the path the plane had taken. He could hardly believe it. Several hundred yards up he saw the broken tops of trees, then the swath cut by the hurtling plane. He saw where they lost the first wing, then where they had hung briefly before dropping. He saw the rocky clearing where they had bounced, and where they had spun, and then the pathway the plane carved when it slid the rest of the way down. He only hoped all that would be visible from the air, in case Bime or Yawsikor sent out a search party.

Somewhere up the mountainside were Dr. Howlett and Kate. But the first one he had to think about was Dad. He didn't know whether his dad was dead or alive, but he knew one thing for sure: He wasn't about to leave his own father in a sweltering box of steel in the middle of nowhere.

CHAPTER 6

Getting to Work

Above all else, even more than the intense feelings of fear and grief, Chad felt alone. He had been crammed inside a small plane with his whole family and a new friend, and now he was afraid he was the only one left. He had no idea where he'd find Kate or Dr. Howlett. But his first task was to somehow get Dad out of the wreckage.

Chad stepped to the front of the plane. Dad was obviously unconscious, but was he breathing? Chad fought tears as he leaned in and pressed his head against his father's chest. There it was! A faint heartbeat! Chad jerked back and banged his head on the edge of the window opening, but he didn't even reach to rub it.

He leaned in and took Dad's face in both hands, turning it toward him and looking for other signs of life. He used his fingers to open one eye, but clearly Dad was not conscious, not seeing anything.

Chad put his ear to his dad's nose to listen for breathing, but he heard nothing. What was it they did on TV? Didn't they put a mirror under the nose to see if any vapor formed? Chad wondered if a piece of shattered window glass would work just as well. He leaned in over his dad and grabbed a piece from between the seats. He held it under Dad's nose and waited. Sure enough, Dad was breathing. It was very slow and seemed weak, just like the heartbeat, but his dad, at least for the moment, was alive.

"Dad!" Chad cried. "I'm gonna need your help!" He wanted

to slap his dad's cheek and get him to wake up, but he had to be careful; he didn't want to make any injuries worse. "I have to know where you're hurt!" Dad did not move.

Chad hurried to the other side of what was left of the plane and searched for anything he could use to wake his dad. Had all their distilled water bottles been thrown from the plane? He finally found one under the other front seat. It had been punctured and was nearly empty, but a few inches of lukewarm water remained at the bottom. Chad splashed it in Dad's face, but nothing happened.

He had feared his dad was dead, and now it looked like he was going to die if Chad didn't do something! He crouched on the seat next to his dad, staring at this man who looked so broken. His head hung motionless, dripping water. With a sudden inspiration, Chad leaned close and blew in his dad's face. As hot and muggy as it was in the jungle, air on water would have to create a change of temperature on the face.

It worked. His dad stirred.

"Dad, wake up!"

Dad's eyes slowly opened, and he winced in pain. He tried to speak, but he could form no words.

"Dad! It's Chad! We crashed!"

Dad struggled to bring his hands to his face, but only his left arm was working. He wiped off his mouth and turned to stare at Chad.

"Dad! Can you hear me? Where are you hurt?"

"K-K-Kate?" Dad managed in a whisper.

"I don't know yet! She was thrown from the plane. Dr. Howlett, too. Tell me where you're hurt and let's get you out of here. I can—"

But Dad cut him off. "Kate," he rasped. "Find Kate!"

"I don't think she made it, Dad. We have to get you to where you can breathe better."

Dad took several seconds to form his words. "I'm okay. Are you hurt?"

"I feel awful, but nothing's broken," Chad said. "Where do you hurt?"

Dad sighed and his shoulder slumped again. It was as if talking at all was too much for him. Chad called out to try to keep him conscious. His dad reached across his body with his good hand and pulled Chad close.

"Chad," he said slowly, then took a breath, "I'm hurt bad all over. I think both my legs are broken. You may not be able to get me out of here, but you've got to find Kate. If she survived, you have to let her know where we are and help her."

"But you can't stay here like this."

"Just put something behind my back so I can sit up straighter and breathe."

"Like what?"

"Anything."

"Everything was thrown from the plane. There's nothing soft. How about these earphones?"

Dad moved his eyes; Chad guessed he was unable to turn his head. "Did you have a water bottle?"

"Part of one."

"Try that."

Chad helped his dad sit forward so the bottle could slide down behind him. Dad's scream as he moved was the most painful thing Chad had ever heard. He knew now what it meant to wish someone else's pain was your own. Dad had always been the strong one. When he was hurt, he never showed it. He had nearly cut off a finger on a table saw once, but he had actually smiled on the way to the emergency room.

"Dad, will you be okay for a few minutes?"

"There'll be plenty of time for me," Dad said. "But listen, Spitfire. If anything happens to me—"

"Don't say that. You're not going to die."

"I'll try not to, buddy, but we can't play games anymore. If anything happens to me, you and Kate and Dr. Howlett need to try to get the radio rigged up and get a message out."

"I don't even know where the radio is!"

"It's right here."

"But it can't be working."

"I'll check it. You go look for them."

"Dad, you—"

"Go!"

It was so painful to watch Dad try to talk that Chad was almost glad to get away from him for a while. On the other hand, he was scared that without him there for encouragement, Dad might give up fighting.

As Chad headed up the path the plane had taken, he felt as if every bone in his body had been crushed. He was stiff and sore and he limped on both feet. He felt pain in his feet, his ankles, his knees, his hips, his back, his neck, his arms, and his head. *What else is there?* he wondered.

Chad climbed about a hundred feet, pulling himself up slowly and painfully by grabbing foliage. He didn't know what kind of creatures to expect in this jungle, but he knew he didn't want to step on anything that would bite. Until he found something to wear on his feet, he would move very slowly.

Chad couldn't help stopping every so often to listen, for what he didn't know. A cry from Kate? A shout from Dr. Howlett? Once when he stopped, he heard something. Did these cannibals, the Brazas, have poison dart guns? Spears? Knives? Did they set traps? Or would they just surround him or run him over in a pack?

What was that noise? Footsteps? The wind in the leaves? The jungle was so moist and hot that Chad welcomed even the slightest breeze. And then he saw it. About twenty feet up the path, in an area that had been cleared by the plunging plane, a wisp of a breeze was gently flapping what appeared to be pages.

Chad quickened his pace. This must be something from the plane. He couldn't imagine anyone ever having been in this part of the jungle before. The clearing was just a ten-foot shelf, a leveling in the mountainside. It was where the plane must have hit that last time, throwing out Dr. Howlett.

Chad reached the source of the faint noise. It was Dr. Howlett's well-worn Bible. The years he'd spent in this climate had dried the cover and made it crumble. The book's spine was broken, maybe by use or maybe due to the plunge from the plane.

Chad knew he needed to continue his search for Kate and Dr. Howlett, so he closed the book and set it down. The slight breeze made him shiver. He felt an urgency to hurry, but he was in so much pain he found it difficult to move.

Where were they and what position was the plane in when Dr. Howlett was thrown clear? Chad guessed that Dr. Howlett had flown through the opening on the left side of the plane. He looked in that direction and saw one of Dr. Howlett's hiking boots, the sock still inside. Crazily, the boot was upright. Chad walked further and saw another boot, only this one was pointed toe-upward, as if worn by someone lying on his back. Which Dr. Howlett was.

Chad had seen only two dead bodies before. One was at the funeral of a classmate who had drowned. The other was his mother's, also at her funeral. He mustered his courage and checked for a pulse on the man's wrist and at the pressure point in his neck. He bent low to listen for breathing, too. Nothing.

Dr. Howlett, Chad knew, was probably crushed by the shifting cargo the first time the plane stopped. Chad wondered if he should come back and bury the man later. It would be the only right thing to do. But for now, he unlaced the remaining boot and carried it over to the other one. He sat awkwardly and put them both on. They were several sizes too big, of course, but he could move much better now. He hoped he would find his own hiking boots somewhere up the path; more than that he hoped he would find Kate—alive.

Chad was tempted to call for her, or to call down to Dad to make sure he was all right. But he didn't want anyone else to hear. Who knew how close a Braza village might be?

He figured Kate might have been thrown from the plane at least another hundred feet up the side of the mountain. He hadn't actually seen her fall, but he recalled that she was missing before Dr. Howlett was thrown. Chad started the difficult, slippery trek up, raising his painful legs high on each step so the long soles of Dr. Howlett's boots would not drag on the mountainside.

About forty feet away from the path, down a tricky ravine, Chad spotted two cargo boxes, still intact, and the cooler Dr. Howlett had bragged about. He'd been right. After dropping from the plane, it hadn't even broken open. Chad only wished he and his family and Dr. Howlett had been as fortunate.

About twenty-five feet farther up the mountain were two more huge crates, but these had split open and cargo was strewn about. One left a trail of things for several yards. Chad didn't bother to see what it all was. If by some miracle Kate had survived, he wanted to get to her as soon as possible.

Chad felt his heart racing and his lungs heaving, and he stopped to rest. He was dizzy and exhausted, the climb in his condition took more from him than he realized. It had been only minutes since the crash, and he had seen more horror and tragedy than ever before in his life. It was too much to take in, too much to think about.

Chad wanted to call out for Kate. Who knew how far from the path she might have been flung? In the silence he heard only his own breathing. He became frantic to get back to his dad. He waited for his breath to return and his pulse to slow, then he set his sights toward the gouge in the trees where the plane had first begun to come down. Kate had been in the plane for several hundred feet past that. Unless she had been thrown so far that he couldn't see her, she would probably be on one side or the other from that point downward.

Chad bent at the waist and set his shoulders forward, trudging up the mountain and grabbing leaves and branches as he went. It wasn't long before his breathing became labored again and his throat grew dry, but he didn't want to stop. He wanted to find Kate so at least he could tell Dad something.

It would be bad enough to return with the report of the death of Dr. Howlett. He hoped against hope that he could tell Dad he'd found his sister—alive.

Suddenly, Chad stopped dead in his tracks. Something caught his ear again. In the stillness he heard movement in the underbrush. This was no rattling paper, no breeze in a clearing. Something was moving, something bigger than a small animal.

"God," Chad prayed silently, "please don't let that be a cannibal. Not now!"

CHAPTER 7

First Things First

C had carried nothing with which he could defend himself. Maybe he should have picked through that strewn cargo. He didn't know yet whether this animal, or Braza, or whatever it was, had seen him. Fortunately, if he could sneak quietly enough, there were plenty of places to hide. The movement came from his right, so he stepped quickly to the left, away from the narrow clearing cut by the crashing plane.

Chad crouched in the underbrush, panting, but trying to keep quiet. Was it a war party? He didn't even know if the Brazas had such a thing. But what would he do if they surrounded him? He was no match for a seventh grader with a snowball, let alone a cannibal in the jungle! Now he saw movement in the leaves across the way. He prayed that whoever it was did not have friends to sneak up from behind, or drop from the trees, or jump from the grass.

He held his breath as the form emerged into the path. It was Kate! She stopped and turned one way and then the other, as if looking for something or someone.

In tennis shoes, shorts, and pullover top, she had scrapes all over her body. Pieces of bark and green stains covered her legs and arms and face.

Chad hurried over to her. He wanted to hug her, but he was afraid if he did, he might make any injuries worse. He could tell by her face that she was delirious, dazed, and confused.

"Oh, hi Chad," she said, as if she had just run into him at school. "Do you know where Mom is? I can't find my parka anywhere."

"Your parka!" Chad almost shouted. "Kate, it's a hundred degrees out here!"

"Mom doesn't want me out without my parka and my gloves." She looked down and stamped her foot. "And these aren't my boots! Where are my boots? Are those my boots you're wearing?"

"These are Dr. Howlett's," Chad spoke more softly. "Kate, you're hurt. You'd better sit down."

"I'm not hurt," she whined. "I'm just cold, and Mom's gonna be mad at me."

"Come with me," Chad said. "We'll find your coat."

He took her hand and held it securely as they carefully made their way back down the mountain.

"This isn't our yard, is it?" she asked.

"No, it's not," Chad said. "Do you know where we are, Katie?"

She shook her head. "Nope."

Chad knew she couldn't deal with it right then. After a bit, they stopped to rest and Chad took a closer look at her. She must have been thrown right into a tree, face first, and slid to the ground. The force had driven tiny branches and twigs and bark into her body. Who knew what kind of injuries she might have? She had probably been unconscious until just before they met. Chad couldn't believe she had been thrown from a plane and was now walking. He wondered how long that would last.

When they reached the area where Chad had found Dr. Howlett's body, he distracted her. "Oh, look, Kate! Somebody's Bible, right here in the path."

"Probably Mom's," she said. "Where *is* Mom?"

Chad slipped and let go of Kate to keep from pulling her down. He didn't want to hurt her any more. He grabbed the Bible and struggled to his feet as she stared at him.

"What happened to you?" she said. "You've got bruises all over."

"We were in a plane crash, Kate," Chad said. "Do you remember?"

"No. Dad's in the war in the desert. Mom's going to pick us up from school, and we're going to go get him at the airport."

Chad put his hand gently on her shoulder. "Kate. Listen to me. Do you know where we are?"

"No."

"Mom's in heaven, remember?"

That seemed to reach her. Kate stood still, squinting as she tried to make sense of it all. "Mom was in an accident," she said.

"Yes," Chad said. "Now you remember."

"The drunk guy didn't stop at the red light. He killed Mom before she even picked us up from school."

"That's right. Dad got to the airport and we were there without Mom, remember?"

She nodded and began to cry. "The policeman told him. It was supposed to be a big happy time, but he was crying. Chad?"

"What, Katie?"

"I think I'm hurt."

"We're all hurt, Kate. Dad's hurt too. We're going to go see him right now, okay?"

She said no more. She just took Chad's hand again and stumbled down the slippery, grassy, rocky pathway. Dad still sat in the plane, rigid with the empty water bottle behind him. He tried a weak wave with his good hand.

"I'll bring her to you in a minute," Chad called. "She's sort of got amnesia, and she's hurt."

Chad noticed Kate limping. The shoe on her right foot looked tighter, as if her foot was swelling.

"Let's get that shoe off," he said, and he sat her down. By now her foot was so swollen that the laces were hard to untie. He struggled to slip the shoe off, then peeled off the sock.

Oh, man! Chad thought. *What am I supposed to do about this?*

All the toes on her right foot were swollen, and he figured they must be broken. He didn't want to be there when she began to feel that pain. "You stay right here, you hear?" he said.

Chad limped over to his father. "We've got to get you out of there," he said.

"I want to see Kate," Dad said.

"She really shouldn't move," Chad said.

Dad winced as he tilted his head to get a look at Kate. "She looks awful," he said in that gravelly voice. Chad told him of her obvious injuries and of his theory that she had slammed into a tree. "Probably right," Dad said. "I'm so sorry, Chad."

"*You're* sorry? This wasn't your fault."

"I know. I'm sorry about all you're having to do by yourself."

"I don't have any choice. I'm the only one who can move much."

"Did you find Dr. Howlett?"

"He's dead."

"Oh, no. How will we ever tell his wife? They've been married more than forty years."

"*When* will we ever tell his wife, Dad? We're not getting out of here."

Dad turned slowly to look directly at Chad. Every word was a chore. "Come here and listen to me," he said. "We're not going to give up ever, are we?"

Chad shook his head.

"Are we?" Dad repeated.

"No, sir."

"Say it like you mean it. Nothing less than our best will get us out of here."

"It's impossible!"

"Nothing is impossible. You know that. God spared us for a reason. I can't believe He would let us survive that crash, only to die a few days later."

"I can't believe that either, but I can't do this! You know I'm no outdoorsman! We're—"

"Chad, what have I taught you all your life?"

"I know."

"Tell me!"

"To be a can-do person, not a can't-do person. But this—"

"I know this is the biggest test anyone could ever face, Spitfire. But either we're going to make it because we're determined to do everything God gives us the strength to do, or we're going to be quitters. Chad, I can't move. All I can do is help you decide what to do. But I promise I'll do my part if you'll do yours. I promise I won't give in or give up. We all need each other. Let's beat this. What do you say?"

"I'll try, but what can I do? I'm hurt too."

"Start with anything that's life-threatening. Do you have any injuries that are going to kill you?"

"I don't think so."

"Any broken bones?"

"Maybe, but they all seem like sprains."

"Anything that needs to be wrapped or braced?"

"Probably, but what will I do that with?"

"We'll have to find something. It sounds like you just got knocked around pretty good. You'll be sore for a long time, but you're not critically injured."

"It won't be long before Kate won't be able to walk."

"Then deal with her next."

"Dad, I don't even know where to start."

"Now you're talking."

"I am?"

"Yes, that's what I want to hear. When we start wondering where to start, that's when we start prioritizing. You remember what that means?"

Chad nodded. "Deciding what to do first."

"Right. Now, what time is it?"

"My watch is gone," Chad said. "What does yours say?"

Dad slowly brought his left arm up in front of his eyes. "Unless this has stopped, it's almost eight-thirty in the morning."

"It seems like we've been here all day," Chad said. "It's hot already."

"It'll get hotter, believe me, especially here. The first thing you have to do is get me out of this little seat. It's getting hot in here, and I feel like I'm getting dehydrated."

"How am I gonna get you out of there?"

"Well, you're going to ignore my screams, for one thing. The way it hurt when you put that bottle behind me is nothing compared to what I'll feel when you drag me across the other seat and onto the ground. I'll try to help you with my left hand, but it's going to take some leverage and some pulling. You'll have to do it, no matter what I say or do. Then, once you get me set up under some kind of shelter, I can tell you what to do next."

"What should I do about Dr. Howlett?"

"You will have to bury him before the sun gets too high in the sky. We don't want animals getting to him."

"Or cannibals."

"I wouldn't worry about them just now."

"Why not? They can't be far away."

"I don't think they'd come to investigate a racket like we made, do you?"

Chad shrugged. "How am I going to bury a big man like that?"

"Spitfire, you have to quit asking me how you're going to do all this stuff. You'll do it, with God's help, because you're the only one who can. You're going to round up all the cargo you can find and set us up a little stash of supplies. And somewhere, somehow, you're going to find or make the tools you need to do what you've got to do. One thing I'm sure of: You'll sleep well tonight."

Kate limped over to them.

"Kate!" Chad scolded. "I told you to stay put!"

"But I'm hurt! What happened?" Suddenly she began sounding like herself.

"It's all right, Chad," Dad said. "Katie, listen. Chad's gonna pull me out of here, and you'll hear me scream in pain. I promise I'll feel better when it's over, all right?" She nodded. "And you're going to be brave for me, okay?" She nodded again, but Chad didn't think she thought things were okay any more than he did.

In less than half an hour, Chad had been through more than anyone, let alone a kid, should have to go through in a lifetime.

But there was more work to do. Dad was right. He had to do the toughest stuff first, and he had to do it soon.

Getting Dad out of the destroyed plane was even harder than he'd expected. The plan was to pull him out on the right so Dad leaned over on the front passenger seat. "My right arm is obviously broken, so be careful of that. My legs may be broken too, but I can't feel them. I don't know how we can avoid hurting my hip. I'll try pushing and pulling with my left arm, and I want you to drag me by my belt until you can get a grip on one of my legs."

It seemed to take forever, and as Dad had predicted, he screamed in pain with every move. But every time Chad hesitated or let up, Dad yelled, "Keep going! Keep going!"

Dad had begun by leaning over and pushing himself away from the left side with his good arm. Then, once he was on his back on the right seat, Chad put his hand under his father's good shoulder and grabbed his belt. He jerked and yanked until Dad's torso was almost out one side of the plane and his mangled legs were in the pilot seat. With a surge of energy, they worked together until Dad flopped out onto the ground, his legs still up in the doorway.

"Dad, I'm killing you!" Chad said.

"Leaving me in there would kill me," Dad said, the pain clearly showing on his face. He used his good hand to try to hold his hip in place as Chad took his feet and pivoted his body free of the plane. "Now, if you can just get me over by that tree, I can stretch out."

It took Chad several minutes to drag his father, from under his arms, across the ground until he had situated him with his back against a tree about fifty feet from the wreckage.

"Get Kate situated near me. Then you've got to start carting the cargo down here. Anything you can salvage, we'll probably need. If you find any pieces of the fuselage up there that you can handle, they might make a good lean-to."

By the time Chad left Dad and sister to head up the mountainside again, Kate lay whimpering in obvious pain.

Chad turned his eyes away when he came to where Dr. Howlett's body lay. He had no idea how he would bury him on the rocky mountainside. And how would he ever get that large man down the mountain?

For now, all he had to worry about was finding the cargo. He decided to start at the highest point where he'd seen anything and keep pushing stuff down before him as he went. Just getting up and down the mountain was a chore. He wondered if he could do this.

At the point closest to where the plane first hit the trees, he spotted the radio antenna wire draped high in some branches. He couldn't reach the low end of it, and jumping or climbing a tree was the last thing he wanted to think about it. Maybe he could get to it later if he needed it.

The next thing he found was the top of one of Dr. Howlett's trunks. It was a three-foot by four-foot lid that had broken off its hinges and it would make a perfect sled. He turned it over and loaded it with as many useful items as he could find. He included vine and twigs to use for setting and wrapping sprained or broken bones.

In a duffel bag hanging from a low branch, Chad found some of Dr. Howlett's personal belongings, including a leather belt and a long, heavy, sharp machete. That huge knife might come in handy. He first used it to poke a hole in the trunk lid, then he threaded the belt through the hole, and fastened it. That would keep the trunk from sliding off the path, or all the way down the mountain. Once he got the lid loaded, he used the weight of the sled to help him walk upright, and then he followed it down by hanging onto the belt.

Two other trunks still had side handles attached, so he struggled back up after them. He heaved and pushed them to the path, and then let them slide down the same way. After an hour, with occasional breaks to check on Dad and Kate, Chad made a large pile near Dad. It was everything he could find that had bounced out of the plane.

Among the pile he found his own socks and boots; he had expected to wear them after a soccer game at Yawsikor. They would make it much easier to climb and walk. He also found an extra shirt for both himself and Dad. Dr. Howlett's personal suitcase held lots of clothes and toiletries that would be useful. Kate could wrap herself in some of his clothes to keep warm that night. Chad also found a copy of the wordless book Dr. Howlett had told them about.

He opened the last trunk to find a treasure of snacks and treats! Dr. Howlett had packed a couple of dozen boxes of fruit punch, the kind with straws attached. He also found a dozen bottles of distilled water, six candy bars, and an entire box of individually wrapped packages of crackers and cookies. Chad and Dad decided they could live for days on that alone. But in addition, Dr. Howlett's indestructible cooler contained a Chinese dinner feast that would feed six or eight adults. Everything had spilled and run together, but if they could keep it from spoiling, the Global Air Troubleshooters could make it last for days—if they had to.

"Spitfire, did you find my backpack?" asked Dad.

"Yeah, I found all three of them."

"Great! Mine has a first aid kit in the bottom. There should be some gauze and bandages and even some antiseptic."

Chad helped Dad clean and dress a cut on his side. He also bandaged Kate's many scrapes and cuts. He spent several minutes pulling twigs from her face and arms and trying to clean her up as well as he could. Then he sprayed antiseptic on her forehead and made her shriek.

"Now, Kate," Dad said, "you may not want to watch while Chad and I try to set my broken arm."

After coaching Chad as to how to pull his right forearm from the wrist and elbow until the protruding bone clicked back into place, Dad put a roll of gauze in his mouth to bite on. Tears poured down Dad's cheeks as Chad worked. At one point Dad reached over with his good hand and helped pull on the arm himself. Then Chad bound the forearm crudely with sticks and vine.

"Is he gonna do that to my toes, too?" Kate asked fearfully after they finished.

"No," Dad said, hissing in pain. "We're not sure if they're broken or if they could be set that way even if they are broken."

Kate lay back in the shade, whimpering. Her foot looked horrible, even more swollen. Chad was the only one left who could walk.

CHAPTER 8

Progress

Chad's dad called him close. "It's driving me crazy trying to figure out what went wrong," he said. His throat was still weak and talking sounded painful. "Did you hear that splashing sound before we started to slide?"

Chad nodded.

"That had to be the reserve fuel tank. That means there was a problem in the line. It was either blocked or had a leak. More likely, it was a leak. If there was a block, we never would have gotten out of Bime. There had to be a hole in the line that emptied the first fuel tank, and then when I switched over to the reserve tank, there was already air in the line."

"How could that have happened?"

"I don't know. We were good coming out of Sentani. The landing at Bime was a little rough, and we may have kicked up a stone. I should have checked."

"There was no reason to check, Dad," Kate said weakly. "It wasn't your fault."

Dad pursed his lips and nodded, but Chad knew he blamed himself. To change the subject, Chad told Dad that he had a plan to pull Dr. Howlett's body down the mountain on the trunk lid, the same way he had moved a lot of the loose cargo.

"Chad," Dad said slowly, "you may find this hard to understand right now when so many other things seem so important. But I think Dr. Howlett's family will really appreciate your efforts."

"Why?"

"Well, they will know, just as we know *he is* gone. His body is just a shell he used when he was here. But they love him, and will be relieved to know you did your best. You understand?"

"I think so."

"Just be careful."

With Dad's advice in mind, Chad made the difficult trip back up the mountain, pulling the trunk lid behind him. He hoped Dr. Howlett would not be much heavier than the loads he had followed down already.

Chad was weak and tired and wanted to collapse, but he knew how important it was to see that Dr. Howlett's body was properly buried.

He couldn't even remember exactly how he did it. Maybe he just repeated the process he'd been using all day, but somehow he got Mr. Howlett's body on the trunk lid and down the mountain.

"Bring me Dr. Howlett's Bible," Dad said. "We'll have a little ceremony, then you need to bury him. Not too deep, but deep enough to protect the body from the elements until we're rescued."

"*If* we're rescued," Chad said.

"*When* we're rescued," Dad corrected.

Chad retrieved the Bible and Dad leafed through it, looking for something to say. "Oh, kids," he said, his voice thick with emotion, "look at this."

He showed them the inscription in the front of the book: "To my beloved on our wedding day." It was signed by Dr. Howlett's wife.

"And look," Dad said, "you can't turn to a page anywhere in this Bible without seeing some underlining or a note. We'll have to keep this safe so we can give it to his wife."

Chad told Dad about finding the wordless book. "She's probably got a whole bunch of them," Chad said. "But she might want the one he had in his suitcase when he died."

"She just might," Dad agreed. "Now, before you bury him, let me just say that this was a man who really loved the Lord and loved His Word. I don't know what else we can say about him. I didn't know him well, but I know he was a good husband and father, a missionary statesman, and someone who cared about winning people to Christ. Let's pray.

"Lord, thank you for the privilege of knowing Dr. Howlett. We know he is with you right now, because that is what your Word promises. Comfort his family when they hear of this. And help us, Lord."

Dad suggested that the grave should be on the other side of the plane, opposite of their little camp. "That way, if the wreckage is spotted from the air, they'll see that you dug a hole and covered it over, and they'll know there were survivors."

"They'll know at least one person died too," Chad said.

"They won't be surprised," Dad answered.

Chad developed blisters on his palms while digging the shallow grave with Dr. Howlett's machete and his bare hands. He knelt on the ground and covered the body with a mound of dirt. The whole time he kept his eyes tightly closed and prayed that this nightmare would soon be over.

He made his way back to where Dad and Kate were half-dozing in the heat. "I have to rest, Dad," he said. He flopped to the ground in a dirty, broken heap.

"I know," Dad said, "but Kate has to give you her ideas about the radio."

"The radio isn't working," Chad said. "It doesn't even switch on."

Kate roused. "The battery cables probably came loose in the crash. If the battery wasn't smashed, it should still work."

"But how do you know it isn't ruined?"

"We won't know until we can get some juice to it," she said.

"Anyway," Chad said, "we're almost three miles down in a valley. The antenna wire is stuck up in the trees."

"Really?" Kate said. "You saw it?"

He nodded.

Kate looked at Dad. "You didn't reel it in before we went down?"

"I was hardly thinking about that."

"I couldn't reach the wire, though, Kate," Chad said. "I'd have to climb a tree to get to it."

"Leave it where it is," Kate said. "What you need to do first is see if the battery and the radio both work. Then you have to get them out of the plane and take them up the mountain to where you can hook the antenna wire to the radio. Having the wire strung out through the trees is probably the best."

"The best for what?"

"For search parties."

"They're not gonna see a little wire in the trees."

"No, but they'll be sending and listening for radio signals. We want our radio to be where they can hear it or reach it."

"Do I have to stay up there by the radio?"

"Not for long," Dad said. "Assuming it even works, we're already past the wind curfews. No one will be flying into or out of Bime until tomorrow morning. We'll be missed at Yawsikor pretty soon, and they'll communicate with Sentani and Bime. It won't be long before Mrs. Coleman lets them know when she heard from us last. She'll tell them we were complaining of fuel gauge problems, so they'll likely start the search just over the divide from Bime."

"Should we have a fire going or spread something out in the trees that they might see from the air?" Chad asked. "We're pretty deep in the bush here."

"You can try putting something up there that they could see, but we'll have to be careful of fires and smoke if we don't want nationals in this area to know we're here."

"The cannibals, you mean?"

"Dr. Howlett himself said there has been no reports of cannibalism for years," Dad said. "But this is the Brazas' area. I can't imagine they even know we're here, but there's no sense frightening them and making it obvious, either."

"But doesn't it get cold here at night? If we can't have a fire, how will we keep warm?"

"The tribal people smear their bodies with pig fat. Short of that, we may have to make some sort of a stove that hides the light of the fire and sends smoke up only after dark."

Chad knew that being seen from the air or heard over the radio were their best and probably only chances of being rescued. Tired and sore as he was, he trudged back to the plane and began pulling sheets of metal from the crumpled sides of the plane. He bent them back and forth until they snapped. When he had a half-dozen pieces of from a foot square to about three feet square, he knew he had enough. He would place them along the path the plane had sheared into the mountainside. Hopefully the sun would hit them and reflect their light to search planes. The search party might see the sheared off wing in the trees, too, but Chad would place these so it was obvious they weren't just the result of the crash. He would shape them in a circle or a cross. That way the searchers would *know* there were survivors.

Kate explained how to remove the radio from the control panel in the cockpit, and Dad said he should find the battery in the nose cone of the plane. "The nose never hit the ground, so the battery may still be in one piece," Dad had told him. "We can hope."

As Chad climbed into the tiny cockpit, which was made even smaller by the crash, he hurt to think about Dad and Kate. Dad had confided to him, when Kate couldn't hear, that any one of the three of them might have serious internal injuries. They might be bleeding inside. What that meant to Chad was that time was everything. Who knew how long they could survive, especially in these elements?

Chad was amazed, as always, at what Kate knew about radios. She was right. He needed no tools to get the radio out of the control panel. There were only a couple of wing nuts to loosen, and one had snapped off anyway. "They make these easy to get out," Kate had said, "because they're easier to work on in the hangar than in the plane."

It was more difficult to get into the nose cone, but when he did, Chad discovered that Kate was right again. All the shaking and rattling around from the crash and slide had jarred the battery loose from the wiring. It was not connected to the radio or anything else on the control panel, and it was far from the long-dead engines.

The battery was heavy, and Chad could hardly budge it. A short, plastic lifting belt was built into it, but even with both hands he couldn't lift it up the two feet he needed to, to get it out of the nose cone. He noticed then that part of the metal nose was on hinges, and it appeared that a huge crease along the other side could possibly be bent again and again until the cone was split in two pieces.

One piece could probably be molded into a perfect small furnace. The other might be straightened and be the beginning of that lean-to his father had suggested. These thoughts were encouraging, but even so Chad was overcome by fatigue. His head ached and his joints seemed to cry out. He slumped to the ground, his back resting against the plane. How could he go on like this? He wanted to trust God, and he wanted to believe it was possible to survive. But he could only do so much. He knew Dad and Kate would help if they could, but since they couldn't, it seemed their survival and rescue depended on him.

He looked forward to showing Dad the pieces of the nose cone, as soon as he could muster the strength to tear them apart. And even though that would make the battery easier to get to and drag out of the plane, how would he ever lug both the battery and the radio all the way up the mountain, and attach the radio to the antenna wire? He would have to use Dr. Howlett's belt again, but would it damage the battery to drag it along the ground? He'd have to use the trunk lid again as a sled. There seemed to be solutions for everything, but that didn't make his job any easier.

As he sat thinking, he felt his body wanting to shut down. If only he could take a nap. Didn't he have until early the next morning to rig up the radio anyway? Maybe if he could make the furnace, shape the lean-to, and make sure the battery worked, then maybe he could take a break. But could he last till then?

Suddenly he spotted a long, narrow plume of smoke rising

on the horizon two or three miles away. That had to be a cooking fire, and it could only be coming from the Braza settlement.

He knew they were there, but did they know his family was here? In that instant Chad realized time was one luxury he could not afford. There was a lot of work to do, and it had to be done now. He made it his goal to create an invisible source of heat, make a shelter from the wind, prepare some sort of a meal, get the radio functioning, and get it up the mountain to the antenna wire, all before dark.

Come dawn and the early morning flights out of Sentani and Bime, he wanted to be on the radio and visible from the sky. He also knew they had to avoid being visible from the ground. Could it be done?

CHAPTER 9

News

C had started building their shelter with the cargo he found. After several trips back and forth to the plane, he finished the job by reshaping one half of the nose cone and building a little furnace out of the other half.

Dad was impressed and said so, but Chad was uneasy about saying much. He had made a difficult decision. He had decided not to tell Dad or Kate about the smoke he had seen on the horizon. And the jerry-rigged lean-to, made from airplane skin, nose cone, and a variety of trunks, backpacks, duffel bags, and junk, blocked their view.

Neither of them was doing well, and Chad tried to push from his mind the possibility that one or both of them might die during the night. Dad was right, of course, any one of them might have serious internal injuries. If they weren't hurt so badly, and if one of them could help Chad, maybe they could hold out for a few days. But not this way. Neither Dad nor Kate would improve enough to walk in the next few days. Whatever Chad had to do to get them out of there, he had to do as soon as possible.

Chad pulled the belt out of the trunk-lid sled that had served him so well and took it back to the plane. He threaded it under the plastic carrier on the battery, then fastened the buckle and slipped the other end of the loop over his right shoulder.

The battery was so heavy it made the belt dig deeply into his shoulder. He lowered it to the ground and decided to make sure the battery still worked before he lugged it all over the place. He sat straddling the box and studying it. Just like a car battery, it had negative and positive poles, one black and one red.

How do you know when a battery is still good? he wondered. He pressed his left index finger on the negative pole and felt a tingly sensation. Then he reached for the positive pole with his right hand.

The next thing Chad knew, he was on his back. He had completed the circuit, and the charge had driven his elbows back so fast that his upper body followed and slammed the back of his head on the ground. How stupid. He should have known better than to do that from elementary school science. He certainly didn't need more injuries. This was nothing serious, he was sure, but he was already sore enough before he toppled back.

So the battery was fine. Now, if the radio was okay, the battery should make it come to life. He would need Kate's advice in hooking it up, however. He looped the belt over his shoulder again, carried the much lighter radio and headphones in his left hand, arm extended to provide some balance, and hauled the battery back to their campsite. By now Dad had maneuvered into a prone position on his back and was sleeping. Chad didn't know if that was a good thing or not, but he certainly didn't want to wake him.

Kate was pale and looked weak, breathing heavily. That, Chad knew, was not a good sign. Maybe she had injured a lung, or maybe there was other damage. He couldn't know. And he didn't know how to help her anyway. "Maybe you should be getting some sleep, too," he said.

"I will," she said. "But let's see if that radio works first."

Chad dragged the stuff over by her. Any time she moved,

even to reach and point at something, she winced in pain.

"Just tell me," Chad said. "I can do it."

She patiently walked him through the process for attaching the wires.

"Be careful not to get a shock," she said.

He almost laughed. He wasn't about to admit his stupidity. How strange it was to smile—even briefly—in the middle of all this horror.

Two connections were to be made in an area so small that Chad had to rummage through Dr. Howlett's toiletries to find a pair of tweezers and make the attachments. Once everything was connected, Kate said, "Just flip that switch. If the red light comes on, you've got power."

He did and it did. "Yes!" they said in unison.

"Now," she said, "play with that tuning button. You won't hear anything except maybe some static until you're hooked up to the antenna wire, but that green light will tell you if you've locked onto any strong frequency."

Chad turned the dial until the green light burned faintly. He played it back and forth until the light was solid and bright. "This is good news, right?" he said.

"Best I've had all day. Now click on the microphone like you're going to transmit. If it makes the green light go out, it's probably working, too."

Chad held down the switch on the mike. The green light still shone.

"That's not so good," Kate said. "Check the connection and move it around a little. Keep the switch on."

When Chad pushed the connector in and out or twisted it a little, the green light wavered. "Good?" he asked.

She shook her head. "If it goes completely out, you can be heard. If it just gets faint, you'll sound crackly and faint too. If it goes on and off, they'll catch only a little of what you say. You'll just have to try it. If they can hear you, you'll know. With the headphones on, you'll know right away if you can hear them. Once you get it hooked to the antenna wire, keep it set at the strongest frequency and try calling Bime."

"In the morning, you mean."

"I guess. If there's no one flying until then, there won't be much radio traffic now."

"I'll find out," Chad said. "First, I'm going to get something for us to eat and drink. You think we should wake up Dad?"

"He looks like he's really resting," she said. "Maybe I'll wake him up in an hour or so. It sure is hot."

"Sure is," Chad said.

It felt like over a hundred degrees and as humid as jungles can get. All of their clothes were soaked with sweat.

"Aren't you hurt?" Kate said. "I feel so bad that you have to do all the work."

"Yeah, I hurt, but mostly I'm just tired. I've already worked harder in just this one day than in my entire life."

"No kidding," Kate said, as if that were obvious.

"I sure don't want to go up that mountain again," he said as he dug through the foodstuffs and found some cookies and water. "This won't be very cold. Later, if you and Dad are still hungry, maybe I'll try cooking some of that rice from the cooler."

"You'd better eat, Chad," Kate said.

He nodded and stuffed some cookies into his mouth. Then he took a quick drink of water. It was warm but still quenched his thirst. He felt an almost immediate surge of energy from the cookies. He stood and stretched his sore muscles and joints.

"I'd better get going before I can't move at all," he said. "I'll leave this stuff close enough for Dad to reach when he wakes up."

Chad was tempted to tell Kate what to do if she needed him while he was gone. He knew he could hear her from a couple of hundred feet up the mountainside if she called out or screamed. But he didn't want to give her any ideas. If she called out or screamed at all, the noise would surely bring the Brazas right to the camp. He would just pray they didn't come this way before he got back. Of course, he didn't want them to ever come around, but at least if he were in the camp, he would have the machete. That was something he couldn't carry up the mountain this trip.

Chad believed this would be his last climb of the day, but he had no idea how difficult it would be. The battery pulling at the belt over his shoulder was heavy and painful and awkward enough, but trying to carry the radio, headphones, and microphone was nearly impossible. He was left with no free hand to help him climb.

He wrapped the microphone cord and the earphones around the radio, worrying that he might be damaging them. He tucked the whole mess under his free arm, but he couldn't get any leverage. When he tried to reach with his arm that carried the battery, the belt slipped and the battery swung, and bumped him, knocking him off balance.

Chad felt like giving up, and he slumped in the path for a moment. He stole a glance at the horizon. Now *two* columns of smoke billowed from a mile or two away. He must think of something. He finally decided to suspend the belt over the top of his head and let the battery hang down his back. It was the way he had seen the nationals carry loads. And it was better than making two trips almost straight up hill, more than two hundred feet.

He set the battery down and sat in front of it. Then he reached back and slipped the belt to the top of his head. He pulled his feet up under him and rose slowly, feeling the weight begin to press into his head. Upright now, he felt the battery swing into his back. It felt lighter, balanced in the middle of his body. But he wasn't sure how long he could endure the pressure on his head. He had to hold his neck straight and stiff.

Then Chad squatted down again to pick up the radio. He quickly straightened with the radio in one hand. Now he had one hand free to grab at rocks and branches as he climbed. Every few feet he stopped to adjust the belt. By the time he reached the tree where the low end of the antenna cable dangled, he had stopped several times just to catch his breath.

"Lord," he prayed silently, "I can't do this by myself."

The ground by the tree trunk was at a steep angle and he had to push the battery into the soft underbrush to keep it from sliding or tumbling back down the mountain. He lodged the radio and all the cords on the upside of the tree, then sat to gather his strength before climbing. He had never felt more hot, more sweaty, more exhausted. He remembered the sheer terror of the plunge down the mountain in the plane, but now he felt another deep fear. Could the Brazas be watching and he didn't even know it?

Chad scoped out the tree from where he sat and spotted a fork in the trunk where he could set both battery and radio, if he could get them up there. The antenna wire hung close enough for him to reach if he stretched. He would have to carry the battery on top of his head again, so he could have both hands free for climbing. He decided to climb the tree empty-handed first, and pull the wire into position. The climb was easier than he expected, but the wire was surprisingly tight. He was careful not to pull so hard that the whole thing gave way, and he was finally able to pull the end down to where he could sit and work with it in the fork of the tree.

Chad held his breath then and heaved himself and the battery up into the tree, all in one move. He couldn't wait to get the belt off his head, and he nearly dropped the battery while slipping his head out of the loop. The battery lodged neatly in the fork with a little room left for the radio, if Chad straddled the larger branch.

One more trip down and up the tree with the radio and attachments, and everything was in place. Kate had shown him where to insert the antenna wire to the radio, but he hadn't expected it to be loose. He didn't have a tool to crimp the wire and make it stay, so he grabbed some leaves and stuffed them into the connector. He didn't want to have to wiggle the antenna wire—something he knew he would have to do with the microphone cord. If this whole contraption worked, it would be a miracle.

Chad rigged up the battery to the radio, the way Kate had shown him. When he flipped the switch he got a staticky response. He plugged in the headphones and put them on, then played with the tuner until the light shone bright green. He didn't even plug in the mike, because he didn't expect anyone to be transmitting or receiving at that time of day. No planes had been in the air since 10:30 that morning. He wanted to get his little radio shack set up and tuned in. Then he could turn it off for the night to save the battery, and then be back at the crack of dawn.

In the middle of the static, however, when the green light was clearest, he heard a voice and nearly fell out of the tree. He pressed the headphones closer to his ears as he teetered there on the branch and tried to stay upright by pressing his sore thighs tight against the limb. He couldn't let go of the phones.

"Can you give us an update, Langda, over?"

"What was the latest you heard, Koropun?"

"Only that they should have landed Yawsikor early morning. Left Bime in plenty of time. Last contact was with Bime shortly after takeoff. They could be in this area."

Chad reached for the microphone and nearly bumped the radio out of the tree. He jammed the cord into the unit and pushed the button, shouting, "We're down in the mountains, just the other side of Bime in line with Yawsikor!"

But the green light had never gone off. He knew no one could hear him. He mashed the button again, but he couldn't remember the name of either base. "Hello? Hello? Is anyone there? Mayday! Mayday! Crash site to Bime!"

He jiggled the connection, and even though *he* heard the static, apparently no one else on the air did. He listened some more.

"Mrs. Howlett will be flown into Bime at daybreak, over."

"Roger, we heard that. Several planes from the different agencies will help out. Only a float plane is available from Yawsikor. They will set a course directly toward Bime and fly as low as possible."

"What do you make of no radio contact, over?"

"Not good. There's supposed to be another briefing broadcast at eighteen hundred hours, over."

"Roger and thanks, over and out."

Chad had no idea what time it was now, but he knew eigh-

teen hundred hours was six o'clock at night. He also knew the
sun went down fast in the tropic zone and it would be getting
dark by six. He couldn't wait to tell Dad and Kate. He wanted to
try to make his microphone work again, but with both stations
off line, they wouldn't hear him anyway He wondered what a
briefing broadcast was. Would all the stations be on? He didn't
think Yawsikor could pick up stations on the other side of the
divide, but maybe they relayed messages. Where were the two
stations he had just heard? They had to be on this side of the
divide in order to hear each other and in order for him to hear
them, and they had to be fairly close to Bime if they thought the
plane could be near them.

Chad made sure everything was hooked up and in place.
Then he shut it all off and scampered down the mountain, slipping and sliding, grabbing and falling, but not feeling the pain as
he had before. He knew he would feel it later when he slept—*if*
he slept—and for sure he would feel it in the morning. But for
now, he just wanted to get down and tell Dad and Kate the good
news.

He would round up shiny stuff to stick on the trail, and no
matter what, he would be back to the radio before nine o'clock.
Even if he couldn't make them hear him, he was sure that planes
looking for them between Bime and Yawsikor would spot something.

Finally, he thought. *We're getting somewhere.*

CHAPTER 10

The Attack

Though they weren't in any condition to jump around, Kate and Dad were as excited about the radio transmission as Chad had been. His news was balanced, however, by their news.

"We can't think of any way to start a fire," Dad said. "We have no matches, no flint, nothing."

"How about rubbing two sticks together like the Indians used to do?" Chad suggested.

"Have you ever tried that?" Dad said. "You have to have patience and perfect conditions. Maybe we could use the sun, magnified through Dr. Howlett's reading glasses. We could point it at a cotton ball soaked with alcohol, but then a fire might make it obvious to *everyone* where we are. We know no search planes will be out till tomorrow morning, so the only people we would be signaling might see us as enemies."

"There is a way to start a fire after dark," Kate said, "but I don't think you want to hear it."

"What?"

"You take about an eight or ten-inch piece of the antenna wire and connect the two poles of the battery. It'll shoot out sparks that would ignite dry leaves or paper."

"But how am I supposed to get the fire back down here?"

"You'd have to bring the battery down here to do it," Dad said.

Chad shook his head. There was no way he could unhook

that battery after the six o'clock transmission, bring it down in the dark, and then get it back up there in time to listen for search planes in the morning.

"Isn't there any other way to keep warm tonight?" he managed, finally.

"We can bundle up with the extra clothes from Dr. Howlett's suitcase."

"Will that work?"

"It'll have to."

"I won't be able to cook you any of that Chinese dinner."

"We're not hungry."

It was true; they didn't look hungry. Actually, both Kate and Dad looked awful. Their eyes looked heavy, and they hardly moved at all. Dad was pleased to get some feeling back in his legs, but he still had to use his good arm to move them. Dad's abdomen appeared swollen, but Chad didn't mention it. There was nothing he could do anyway, and surely Dad didn't need to hear more bad news.

Kate's toes were discolored and Dad worried aloud that there might be a blood-circulation problem. "What does that mean?" she asked. "I could lose my toes?"

"You could," Dad said, "but we're going to pray we're spotted first thing in the morning and lifted out of here. Meanwhile, try wiggling your toes as much as you can to keep the blood flowing."

"Dad," Kate said, "my toes won't even budge." She grimaced as she tried to wiggle them.

"You might have to move them with your hand, Kate," Dad said.

She tried, but the pain brought on fresh tears.

"It's important," Dad said. "Do you want Chad to do it for you?"

"No! I'll do it myself." She forced herself to pull her toes back and push them forward with her hand. She cried out in pain, which made Chad instinctively scan the horizon. He quickly caught himself and tried to appear casual, as if he were not looking for anything special.

But then, to his horror, he noticed a cooking fire that was only half the distance away as the ones he'd seen earlier. Either a settlement of Brazas was closer than he thought, or a group was moving toward the crash sight. Could it be a war party?

Chad tried to sound relaxed. "What time is it, Dad?"

"Almost 5:30. You'd better take my watch. You've got to get stuff up in the trees before dark and be by the radio by six."

It was still hot and humid as Chad rustled through the cargo and found lots of Dr. Howlett's clothes. Many of them were dress clothes, including white shirts and even two suits. It seemed strange to be piling them next to Kate and Dad with the sun still so warm. But Chad knew when the sun went down in the mountains, the temperature would drop quickly.

"You'd better take something warm with you too," Dad said.

Chad chose a light-colored denim vest with lots of pockets. It had probably fit Dr. Howlett perfectly, but it hung almost to Chad's knees. He loaded himself up with the sheets of metal from the plane and started, this time for sure, his last trek up the mountain for the day.

After all he'd been through, Chad was amazed he could keep on going. He knew, as his mother used to say, that he was "running on nervous energy." Would he just collapse and sleep when he ran out of gas? Maybe, but there was too much to do first.

Chad climbed up the familiar trail and higher where the plane had plowed through. He carefully arranged the sheets of metal in the form of a cross in each tree. No one in the air could mistake that for crash debris. It would be obvious that someone had put them there, in that shape, on purpose. If searchers saw them, it wouldn't be long before they spotted the plane wreckage with the fresh grave off to one side and the little encampment fifty feet to the other side.

It was getting dark as Chad carefully made his way back to the radio. Sharp pain shot through his muscles, and dull pain seemed to have settled into every joint. His head throbbed, and he was hungry again. At the base of the tree he sat to rest, and thrust his hands into the deep pockets of Dr. Howlett's vest. He felt something small and hard at the bottom of one pocket. A cigarette lighter! Dr. Howlett was not a smoker, but he probably knew that a lighter was handy in the bush.

Chad's fingers quivered as he tried it. It produced a flame on the second spin! He almost cried out in joy. He could surprise Dad and sister and start a fire.

But now, as the sun slipped away and a full moon rose, Chad slowly climbed into position. He checked Dad's watch. In about five minutes the radio briefing would begin. What would be better than getting someone who was listening to hear him? They would be turning on their sets about now, he decided, and so he did the same.

Chad put on his earphones and heard only a faint hiss. He carefully held the end of the microphone cord straight and steady and pushed it into position. When he clicked the thumb switch on the mouthpiece, the green light went out. He blinked, wondering if he were seeing things. He clicked it again, and again until finally the light went out.

If that meant he could be heard, Chad didn't want to wait. He wanted to be on the air when everyone else switched on for the briefing. He watched the green light carefully every time he clicked the button. When it went out completely, he spoke quickly.

"This is the crash site calling. Mayday. Mayday. Crash site, does anyone read me? We're the other side of the divide from Bime and crashed in the valley on course to Yawsikor. Does anyone read? Come in, please!"

Chad waited a minute, listening, then tried again. He looked at his watch. It was a few seconds before six. Soon he heard other stations come on the air and realized that there was some sort of a relay system. The only voices he could hear clearly were from the two stations he had heard earlier, Koropun and Langda. They seemed to be getting messages relayed from Sentani to Mulia and Bokandini and then to Nalca, Eipomek, Bime, and Okbap. One of those stations must have had a transmitter at the top of the divide to communicate with Langda and Koropun.

Chad decided not to interrupt while each station was identifying itself. If his transmission really did work, he didn't want it to get lost in the traffic. Once everyone was on, the operator at Langda begin relaying the messages from Bime, pausing between each sentence:

"Here's the latest at eighteen hundred hours. This is coming directly from Dave Coleman at Bime. Three planes and a search party will arrive Bime as close to oh-five-thirty hours as possible. Mrs. Howlett will be in that party, but will remain at Bime during the search, which will begin at oh-six thirty hours.

"So far there has been no word of sighting from Yawsikor.

No radio contact. As you all know, last radio contact with Pilot Michaels came at about oh-seven-thirty hours with a report of fuel or fuel gauge problem. He was on course to Yawsikor, but no word on where or when they might have gone down."

There was a pause and Chad quickly clicked on. The green light went faint, but he plunged ahead anyway. "Crash site is on the air!" he shouted. "Mayday! Mayday! Does anyone read me?"

"This is Koropun. We temporarily lost you there, Langda. Repeat after no word when or where they might have gone down, over."

"Nothing further on that, Koropun. I lost Bime there for a second, too. Stand by. Here's more from Bime. Coleman says they have had a development. A houseboy disciplined by Howlett and the Colemans heard of the loss of contact with the plane and has confessed to hurling a shovel at the plane while it sat empty on the runway at Bime. This would have been minutes before takeoff. Houseboy is regretful and wants to be involved in search effort. Coleman hasn't decided whether that would be a good idea."

"What damage could have been done, over?"

"Bime, this is Langda. Koropun is asking what damage the shovel might have done, over."

Chad tried cutting in again. "Crash site to Langda or Koropun! Come in, please! Mayday! We lost fuel from the main tank and couldn't get reserve fuel to the engines! Does anyone read?"

"Langda to Koropun, stand by; we're hearing from Bime, but with interference."

"Breaker! Breaker, Langda, this is Koropun. Did you hear—?"

"Stand by, Koropun! Losing Bime."

"Breaker, Langda! Emergency breaker! This is Koropun, and we're hearing from crash site!"

"Koropun repeat, over!"

"Stand by Langda and all stations. Crash site, this is Koropun. Repeat please."

Chad mashed the button and shouted into the microphone. "Mayday! This is crash site!"

"Back off from the mouthpiece a bit there, son. What's your location and situation?"

Chad was so excited he was shaking and couldn't slow his words. "We're in the valley on the other side of Bime!"

"Check your connection, crash site. Repeat please."

Chad tried again, keeping an eye on the green light. It went off completely only for a second.

"All we got was 'valley,' crash site. Survivors?"

"Other side of Bime!" Chad tried again. "Three survivors."

"I didn't get any of that," the voice at Koropun said. "Langda?"

"This is Langda. He said three something. Stand by all stations. Koropun is getting something from the crash site, but it's breaking up. It's a young boy on the radio, and we've got valley for a location and possibly three survivors. Stand by."

Chad kept trying, but the mike connection was bad and getting worse.

"Koropun to crash site, stand by. If you can read us, listen. Your transmission is bad. Hold for a moment."

"This is Langda. Bime says the boy would be the pilot's son. Any word on Dr. Howlett, the daughter, or the pilot?"

Chad tried to break in. "Three survivors!"

But no one could hear anything now. He wrenched the connection around and around, but all he heard was static.

After the word spread throughout the stations that radio contact had been received from the crash site, the operator at Langda tried to summarize. "We've lost the transmission, but we and Koropun will stay on for another hour just in case. We each read a little from the boy, so the site has to be on this side of the divide. Let's assume the best, that Michaels got to the clearings about fifteen minutes past the bottom of the valley and was able to get down somehow. They can't fly out of there, and they can't climb out either, so we'll need to locate them and get a chopper in there. Stand by. Go ahead, Bime."

There was a pause as Langda listened to Bime. "Dave Coleman reminds us that they could be in Braza territory. Crash site, if you can hear us, we have no relationship with that tribal group. They might be unfriendly and violent. Avoid contact, if possible."

Chad tried answering, but the green light stayed on.

"We'll take from those clicks and that static that you can hear us and that you acknowledged that."

Chad clicked several times again.

"We're reading that, crash site. Give me a double click if you read."

Chad double clicked.

"Roger! Work on that radio! We'll stay on the air all night and will monitor this frequency. You'll make it a lot easier on us if you can help us locate you in advance. Give me a double click if you reached clearings and were able to put down safely."

Chad waited.

"Give me a double click if the plane is damaged."

Chad clicked twice.

"Any casualties? Any dead, I mean?"

Chad clicked again.

"Injured?"

He clicked again.

"Son, I'm going to walk you through a series of questions, and by your response you can give us a lot of information. Let's determine who's alive and how serious the injuries are. There's a mission hospital at Angaruk. Then we'll try to pinpoint where you are. Do you read?"

Chad clicked again, but before he heard another word footsteps sounded in the tall grass beneath him. He froze in fear and switched off the radio. But he was too late. Two strong hands grabbed his dangling ankle and jerked him from his perch.

Chad landed hard on his side and felt the air rush from his lungs. The headphones were slipping from his ears, the cord pulling the radio from the tree. He gasped for air, and in the moonlight between the branches, the fierce face of a young tribesman stared down at him. As the warrior reached for his spear, Chad grabbed the earphone cord and pulled with all his might. The radio slipped from the fork in the tree, then hung suspended as it tightened its connection with the battery. Chad tugged again, and the radio pulled free of the antenna wire and dislodged the battery. Radio, microphone, and battery tumbled out of the tree, and the battery smacked the tribesman in the shoulder. He screamed and raised the huge spear high over his head with both hands.

Chad didn't even have time to pray as the heavy spear tip rushed down at him.

CHAPTER II

The Standoff

C had covered his head with his arms and rolled quickly to his stomach, but he was not the target of the tribesman's spear. The spear drove into the radio and smashed it to pieces. His attacker felt the battery with the toes of one foot, then tried to push it out of the way.

Chad knew he could lie there and be killed and maybe even eaten, just as he had taken the snowball attack from the seventh graders, or he could fight for his life, and the lives of his dad and sister. If he hadn't suffered through so much already, he might have remained paralyzed with fright, but now he knew he had nothing more to lose.

He leaped to his feet and faced the tribesman, who now pointed his spear at Chad. He then hefted up the heavy battery and held it in front of him, poles facing the warrior. When he saw the man coil, as if ready to thrust the spear, Chad rushed him and pressed the battery poles right against his bare stomach.

The warrior dropped his spear and fell back, screaming. He spoke quickly in words that made no sense to Chad, then seemed to call out to someone. Chad's heart sank as he heard more footsteps in the dark jungle.

The man bent to retrieve his spear, but Chad thrust the battery toward him again. The warrior backed off a step, so Chad dropped the battery and grabbed the spear. But rather than holding it on his opponent, Chad threw it down the mountain as far as he could. The warrior looked terrified.

Chad picked up the battery again and forced the man to back out into the path created by the crashing plane. Three other tribesmen, also armed with spears, appeared from the other side of the path. Chad's attacker spoke to them quickly, pointing at the battery, and to Chad's amazement, they all threw their spears over his head and down the mountain.

Chad was not sure how long he could stand there holding the battery, but as long as they were scared, he was in control. When he finally set it down and straightened up, he sensed the tribesmen, who he was sure were Brazas, tense again as if ready to either attack or run away. Chad pulled the lighter from his pocket and produced a tiny flame.

The Brazas stumbled back and stood staring at the lighter and then into Chad's face. Now what should he do? They were big, muscular men, barefoot, with huge, wide feet. They wore something at their groins that he could not see clearly, and their stomachs were bound with twine or vines, wide belts so tight that they changed the men's shapes. Blocks of wood stuck out of two of the men's ear lobes, and the other two had bones or sticks through their noses. Chad didn't know what cannibals were supposed to look like, but these four sure seemed to qualify.

It felt so strange to have the advantage, at least for now. Chad's first instinct was to scream out for Dad or sister, but they could do nothing, and he didn't know how many more Brazas were in the area. He knew something they didn't know: If they merely rushed him, they could overpower him easily. Then how long would it be before they discovered Dad and Kate?

For now, they were afraid of the battery, for good reason, and of the flame, because it seemed to appear out of nowhere. Chad knew he had to conserve the tiny supply of butane in the lighter, so he let go and the flame died. But each time the Brazas moved again, he flicked it back on. They were at his mercy. At least for now.

If he charged them and scared them and made them run off, could he and his family hide from the rest of the Brazas until the search planes flew over in the morning? He didn't think he could even stay awake that long. There was no way he would try to fight these people.

The longer they all stood there, and the more he thought about it, the more Chad realized that *he* was the outsider. He was the threat. This area was their home. How would he react if *he* saw an alien in a tree in *his* back yard, talking to and listening to a squawky box?

He still feared that these were dangerous warriors and maybe even cannibals, but he couldn't blame them for attacking him or being scared of contraptions they had never seen before. If only he could remember those words Dr. Howlett had taught him and Kate! Nothing came to mind. He remembered that the words were strange and different and that one of them had sounded to Kate like an ice cream cone.

"Tasty freeze," he said.

The Brazas flinched, wide-eyed, and looked first at him and then at each other. One of them tried to repeat the word, but in his guttural dialect, it was impossible to understand.

Chad knew *tasty freeze* must not mean anything in their language. What *were* those words? And would they have the same meaning twenty-five years after Dr. Howlett and Dave Coleman had met this tribe? If only Chad could remember the greeting, the word for gift, and the word for friendliness. He didn't want to be an enemy of these people. He just wanted to stay alive long enough to be rescued.

What was it Dr. Howlett said the Brazas had called him and Dave Coleman? Yes! George-George and Man-Man!

"George-George," he said.

Again, one of them echoed him, but there was no sign that they had any idea what Chad was saying.

"Man-Man," he said, and this time they didn't even try to repeat it.

"George-George?" he said again, this time as a question. "Man-Man?"

Nothing. Of course, these tribesmen were children or maybe not even born when Dr. Howlett and Mr. Coleman had made contact with that small party years before. They were probably the age now that Jonga was then, the one Dr. Howlett said had taught him and Mr. Coleman a little of their dialect. Could Jonga still be alive? Would any of these men know him?

"Jonga?" Chad tried, and all four men recoiled at once, startling Chad and almost falling over each other. They stared at him in shock. Now he was on to something.

"Jonga!" he said with confidence.

"Jonga!" the four said together. They looked at the one who had attacked Chad. He spoke quickly, obviously running together several Braza phrases and sentences, but Chad understood nothing except for the one name he heard twice. *Jonga.*

Chad repeated it in as friendly a tone as he could. Now the warrior spoke even more quickly and was harder to understand. But he appeared to want to communicate with Chad. His tone was softer and more insistent. Chad held both hands out, the lighter still in one, just in case. He said the name as a question, hoping they would understand that he was asking where the man was.

"Jonga?"

The warrior was excited and moved closer to Chad as he spoke. He pointed to the west. Was it possible Jonga was nearby? Or were they just saying anything they could think of in hopes it would allow them to escape? He didn't want to hold them. But when the warrior stepped still closer, Chad lit the lighter one more time. He couldn't take any chances.

The man stepped back, still afraid of the flame. Chad let it die, and gesturing toward the west, said kindly, "Jonga. Jonga." He nodded and pointed as if urging the men to go get Jonga. Would they bring him back, or would they return with an entire war party?

The four began to move back and step away, keeping their eyes on Chad as if to make sure it was all right that they retreat. He tried to smile at them, though in his fear and fatigue he doubted his smile looked like more than an attempt at a pleasant face. Suddenly the men were running, and he had never seen or heard such speed. Their bare feet flew through the grass and underbrush. The sound quickly faded, and Chad remained in the moonlit silence. He had just stood his ground against four primitive men who might be cannibals.

The problem was, he and his family were at least twelve hours from being spotted by rescuers. His radio was useless. He didn't know if he should tell Dad and Kate what had happened. Why worry them? But if he did tell them, and he wasn't here when the Brazas came back, would the cannibals come looking for him? What if they found him with Dad and Kate? Would he be endangering his family?

He could only guess if he had time to run down to the campsite. At least he could tell Dad and Kate about the radio transmission. But first he climbed back into the tree and grabbed hold of the antenna wire. He measured out about ten inches of it and bent it back and forth until that section broke free. He took it back out into the path and wrapped one end around one pole on the battery. Again he felt the buzzing through his fingers.

Chad left the other end of the wire sticking above the other pole. Then he stood and pressed the wire down with his foot until it touched the pole. Sparks shot into the air and he let up, releasing the contact. Perfect.

He hurried down to the campsite. As he ran, he tried to think of an excuse to leave Dad and Kate again right away. He would tell them about the radio transmission and that the search party would be looking for them at dawn. But he would not tell them of his discovery of the lighter. If he did, they would wonder why he couldn't build them a fire. There was no way he wanted to provide any kind of sight or smell that might lead the Brazas to his family.

Neither would Chad tell Dad or Kate about the Brazas. It would be the hardest secret he would ever have to keep, but he couldn't think of anything good that could come of their knowing. Dad might not let him go back to meet them, and even if he did, what if Jonga did return with the warriors? Dad would worry, as Chad did, that it was a trick. There was no way to know if Jonga was friendly, if he *was* still around after all those years. Men in these tribes didn't live long, so by their standards, Jonga would have to be old even if he were only in his forties.

Besides, there was never any indication that Jonga understood the message Dr. Howlett and Mr. Coleman had tried to tell him. It was foolish to think that Jonga might see himself as a friend to Chad's family, even if they could convince him they were friends of Dr. Howlett.

When Chad got back to the camp, Dad was gravely ill. Chad could see in the moonlight that his abdomen was even more swollen, and his forehead was hot. "I think I've got internal bleeding," Dad said, his voice more raspy than ever.

"What can I do, Dad?"

"I don't think there's anything we *can* do," he said. "I don't even know what kind of medicine is good for this. Besides a bottle of aspirin, we have some antibiotics and penicillin, but I don't think those would do me any good. I don't know how long I have, Chad."

"Can you make it till dawn?" Chad explained to Dad what had happened on the radio. Kate sat up, looking hopeful at last.

"I'll do my best, Spitfire," Dad said. "That'll give me a goal. I don't know how much good it does to just decide to hang on until help arrives, but that's what I'm gonna do. You and Kate pray for me, hear?"

They both nodded.

"Chad," Dad said, "no matter what happens, I want you to know how proud I am of you."

"I know." Chad couldn't help wondering what Dad would think if he knew everything.

"I mean it," Dad said. "If I don't make it, you do everything you can to get Kate out of here. And just know that your dad, and of course your mom, loved you kids more than anything on earth."

"Dad!" Kate said. "Don't be talking like that. If you don't make it, I don't want to make it. So if you want me out of here, you have to stay with us."

"I'll try, Kate."

"Just do it!" she said. "Fight!"

Chad knew he had to get back up the mountain, but he wasn't sure he should leave Dad. On the other hand, there was nothing more he could do for him right now.

"Are you cold, Dad?"

"Yeah, but it feels good with this fever."

"You want *any* medicine?"

"I probably should have antibiotics, but I just don't know if you're supposed to take those when you have internal bleeding."

"How about just some aspirin for your fever and pain?"

"Yeah, maybe that would be good," Dad said.

"No!" Kate said. "You can't have aspirin when you're bleeding. Doesn't aspirin make your blood thinner?"

"You're right, Kate," Dad said. "Good call."

"You're going to make it," she said. "Just try to rest."

"I'm going back up the mountain," Chad said. "I'll be back in a little while."

"You need to rest too," Dad answered. "You've had quite a day."

You don't know the half of it, Chad thought. "I will," he said. "I just want to make sure everything's set for tomorrow." That was as close to lying to Dad as he ever wanted to come. As he pulled the machete from between two cargo trunks, he asked Kate, "What were those Braza words Dr. Howlett taught us?"

"Who cares?"

"I do. You were just about singing them on the plane, and now I can't remember any of them."

Kate sounded as if she were falling asleep. "*Treetzee* means friendly," she mumbled. "*Shaka* means hello. *Benboon* means gift."

"That's right," Chad said casually, running them over and over in his mind. He filled his pockets with packaged cookies, and then slipped the machete into a loop in Dr. Howlett's denim vest. The long blade brushed against the back of his leg as he started up the mountainside, munching on cookies as he went.

About halfway to where he'd left the rigged battery in the path, he looked up into the moonlight and saw at least five silhouettes. One carried a huge torch. Chad could only hope it was the original four spearmen and hopefully a friendly old Braza named Jonga. If it wasn't, then no matter how close he and his family had been to a dawn rescue, they were as good as dead now.

CHAPTER 12

Like Guardian Angels

It was at that showdown moment that Chad almost felt like giving up. His body cried out for rest, for sleep, for healing. Every fiber and muscle and bone ached. And even though he was afraid of the cannibals, and worried that they might attack him, or worse, they might find and kill the rest of his family—all he wanted was an end to all this!

His choice, his hope, his prayer was for this to be a friendly meeting and that somehow he could avoid any violence. But his confused, tired mind could accept even a violent encounter, if that was to be. He knew he couldn't stay awake much longer. His body couldn't work much longer. He couldn't possibly climb this steep, slippery, overgrown mountainside one more time.

Somehow he had to beat the Brazas to the battery. He had the machete, but he didn't want to pull it out. They could just as easily have replaced their spears. If they all threw at him at the same time, he certainly wouldn't be able to defend himself with a cigarette lighter. He might scare them with the sparks from the battery trick, but he had to get to it before they did. And so he quickened his pace.

Chad wanted to run but he could only limp, lurching up the mountain like an old man. From the other direction the torch and silhouettes grew larger and more distinct in the moonlight. There were indeed five tribesmen, and one appeared older and smaller than the others. The younger four carried spears.

The Braza party stopped about twenty feet above the battery. That was good news, because even moving as quickly as he could, Chad was still twice that far below it. The Brazas were bigger, stronger, healthier, and knew how to walk this terrain. While Chad, besides being younger, smaller, and sore all over, still had an uphill climb.

Just to be safe, he pulled out the lighter and lit it as he approached the battery. Though his little flame was no match for their torch, he knew they must still be fascinated and afraid of a little flame that could magically appear in a boy's hand.

The Brazas just stood and stared. If they whispered among themselves, Chad couldn't hear them. He was tempted to push down on the battery wire with his foot, just to show them a shower of sparks and let them know he still had that strange power. Instead he prayed silently to know what to do. He felt that he should just stand there and wait. He snuffed his light and put the lighter in his pocket.

Without a word, the stooped, older Braza stepped away from the others and walked slowly toward Chad, stopping about ten feet from him. Chad stepped to the left side of the path, which made the old Braza turn and face him from the other side. That also allowed Chad to get a look at his face in the moonlight.

It was a face of fear and confusion, but also of some strength. What looked like a bone or stick had been pushed through his nose horizontally. The Braza held his hands out before him, palms up, and spoke softly in a high, nasal pitch. "Jonga," he said.

Chad was startled. He pointed at the man, which caused the Braza to take one step back. "Jonga?" He wanted to apologize for scaring him by pointing at him, but he knew no words for that.

"Jonga," the man said again.

Chad pointed to himself and patted his chest. "Chad," he said.

"Dahk," the man said.

"Chad," Chad repeated.

"Chahk," Jonga said.

"Close enough," Chad said, smiling. Jonga looked confused. "Shaka," Chad said.

The old man flinched. He looked quickly to his companions and then back at Chad.

"Shaka," Chad repeated, and the old man smiled.

"Shaka, Chahk," he said.

"Shaka, Jonga," Chad said. "Treetzee."

"Treetzee?" Jonga said, his whole body seeming to loosen up.

"Shaka, Jonga!" Chad said. "Treetzee!"

Jonga bowed slightly, and he repeated, "Treetzee."

Suddenly Chad remembered the cellophane wrapped packages of cookies in his pockets. He put both hands in his pockets, and Jonga retreated, obviously frightened.

"No, no!" Chad said. "Um, ah, benboon! Benboon!"

Jonga eyed him warily as Chad pulled out the packages. He held one out to Jonga, who hesitated. "Benboon, Jonga. Benboon."

Jonga accepted the package, turning it over and over in his hands as he studied it. Chad, in his enthusiasm, tossed four more packages to the others up the pathway. They jumped away and stared at them as they fell to the ground.

"Benboon!" Chad said, and all eyes turned to him once more. "Look, or I mean...well...watch, whatever. Benboon, treetzee!" He opened his own package and ate one of the filled cookies. "Mmm," he said, hoping they would understand.

The younger men crouched and looked at the cookie packages but didn't touch them. Jonga tried to open his. Chad stepped toward him, causing Jonga to stiffen again and the warriors to straighten up and step forward.

"Here," Chad said, "let me show you. Um, treetzee." Chad slipped a fingernail under the cellophane and tore it away from the cookies. Then he stepped back and let Jonga finish opening them. Chad realized that just because he had shown them the cookies were edible didn't mean they would trust him, or the cookies. It could be a trick, a trap. These were primitive people, but not stupid.

Chad put another cookie in his mouth and gestured to Jonga, but the older man would not eat his. "George-George," Chad said suddenly.

Jonga nearly stumbled in surprise. He looked as if he wanted to sit down. He stared at Chad and spoke quickly. It was all jibberish to Chad except "George-George."

Chad nodded and repeated the name. Jonga was excited, and when Chad said "Man-Man," Jonga dropped to his knees, the cookies falling from his hands. He reached to the sky as if celebrating hearing those names again. He stood quickly, then, and pulled the small stick or whatever it was from his nose, holding it out to Chad.

Chad didn't want to touch it, but Jonga was holding it toward the light and pointing at it. Chad looked closely. It wasn't a stick or a bone at all. It was the bottom portion of a plastic ball point pen. The clicker and the ink and point were gone; just the barrel remained. Jonga pointed at the printing on it. Chad leaned close.

Jonga pointed at letters that spelled out Inter-Indonesian Missions, but he said, as if reading, "George-George." He looked up at Chad with a sparkle in his eye. "George-George benboon," he said, and thrust the pen back through the hole between his nostrils.

Chad now knew for sure that this was the very man Dr. Howlett and Mr. Coleman had talked to so many years before. How he wished he knew more than three words in their language!

Jonga rose and picked up the cookies. "Ah loo," he said. "Ah loo. Jeshuz. Gawd."

Chad squinted at him, and Jonga repeated. "Ah loo, Jeshuz. Gawd."

Chad understood that he was trying to say Jesus and God, but what was *ah loo.* "Ah loo?" Chad asked him.

Jonga transferred the cookies to his left hand and thrust out his right, as if he wanted to shake hands. So it was "Hello"! Chad hesitated. If he shook hands with the old man, he would give him an advantage. He could be wrestled to the ground, and be at the mercy of the four warriors. He moved closer to the battery, just in case.

Chad put out his hand, and Jonga reached for it. But rather than shaking Chad's hand, he let his hand slip up to Chad's wrist. As they clasped wrists, Jonga smiled and said, "Ah loo, Jeshuz. Gawd. Gawd blesh choo."

"Hello, Jonga," Chad said. "God bless you, too." So Dr. Howlett and Mr. Coleman had taught the Brazas a few English words while trying to learn their language.

Jonga put the cookies in his mouth and chewed slowly, smiling. The spearmen dropped their weapons and grabbed at the cookies, crumbling them as they tried to open the packages.

Jonga held his arms wide, hands open. "George-George?" he said. "Man-Man?"

Chad didn't know what to say. How could he tell him that Dr. Howlett was dead, but that Mr. Coleman was just over the mountain and would likely be there by morning? He tried to avoid the bad news. "Man-Man," he said, pointing over the mountain. Jonga and the others turned and looked up the path. "No!" Chad shook his head and pointed farther.

Jonga looked puzzled. "George-George?" he asked again.

Chad motioned for Jonga to follow, then he turned to head down the path. He looked back to see Jonga hesitate and look at his companions. Chad motioned for them again. "Treetzee," he said, and he began the treacherous trip down the mountain. How he hoped this was his last time ever!

Chad turned and saw Jonga and all four spearmen walk way around the battery, keeping an eye on it as they passed. He felt weak and alone as he led them to the valley floor. Except for the machete dangling from the loop in Dr. Howlett's vest and the tiny lighter in his pocket, Chad had nothing with which to defend himself. He had chosen to trust Jonga and his friends. He had read stories of missionaries who were slaughtered by hostile tribes, so all he could do was pray silently.

When they reached the bottom of the path the plane wreckage came into view. "George-George?" Jonga said. Chad nodded sadly.

The warriors held out the torch and looked closely at the plane. Surely they had seen the metal birds flying over through the years, and these men may have even seen the helicopter that was turned away when they were children. But they had never seen wreckage like this.

Jonga peered inside the plane. "George-George?"

Chad knew then that he would have to show him the grave to make him understand. He motioned for Jonga and the others to follow. When they got to the mound of dirt over the shallow grave, Chad pointed and said, "George-George."

Jonga put both hands on his stomach and grimaced, rocking on his heels, looking from Chad to the grave and back again.

Chad pointed straight up and said, "George-George. God. Jesus."

Jonga appeared to understand now, but he looked so grief-stricken that Chad wanted to get him away from the grave. At that moment he decided he would introduce Jonga and his friends to Dad and Kate. Once again he motioned for them to follow.

They passed the wreckage again on the way to the pile of cargo trunks and the makeshift lean-to. Jonga and the warriors hesitated as the torch shone on the pile of stuff. Then, as they came around to the other side and saw the two sleeping figures, bundled in layers of clothing, they were startled.

Dad and Kate were sound asleep. Chad went first to Dad, who lay on his back, his breathing labored, his abdomen protruding. It wouldn't have surprised Chad if Dad stopped breathing at any moment.

Kate lay on her side, curled up to keep warm. Chad had to put his ear near her face to hear her breathing. He could only guess that in the absence of medical help, sleep was what was best for them.

Jonga seemed to understand that this was Chad's family, and he had to assume they were all in the plane crash, for what he did next astounded Chad. Jonga seemed to take over. He knelt close to Chad and spoke earnestly, though Chad understood not a word of it.

As Chad watched, Jonga lifted the tiny, cold furnace that Chad had shaped from the nose cone of the plane and tossed it aside. With his hands he swept the area clear and softly gave instructions to his friends. Three of them ran off into the darkness, returning in minutes with twigs and dry leaves and larger pieces of wood. These he piled quickly into a pyramid, then touched the torch to it, and a campfire burst into flames. Even with the light and the heat, neither Dad nor Kate awoke.

Chad had an idea, so he rummaged through Dr. Howlett's belongings and came up with his Bible. "Jonga," he said, holding it out to him, wondering if he had ever seen Dr. Howlett with it. From the puzzled look on his face, it appeared Jonga had not seen the Bible before, but as Chad fanned the pages, the colored pages of the wordless book tucked into the back caught Jonga's eye.

Jonga grabbed it and spoke excitedly, showing his friends. He turned to Chad, pointed to the gold page, then pointed up. "George-George?" he said.

Chad nodded.

Jonga spoke to two of his friends, and they ran off into the night, one with the torch and both with their spears. About half an hour later one returned with a small wild boar he had killed. With his bare hands he ripped off its skin and propped it over the fire. Despite the cookies, Chad had never been so hungry.

About fifteen minutes later the other tribesman returned with Jonga's decades-old, dog-eared copy of the wordless book. Jonga handled the book's pages—now separated into individual sheets with no staples—carefully, as if each one were a prized possession.

A little more than an hour later, Jonga began pulling strips of pork off the boar—again with his bare hands—and everyone who was awake ate. To Chad the meat was as good as the best pork roast his mother had ever cooked.

After they had eaten, Jonga sat near the fire with his legs crossed, the wordless book in his lap. He had apparently instructed his friends to stand guard; they stood at each corner of the little camp, facing out like guardian angels, leaning on their spears.

Jonga pointed to the ground, seeming to urge Chad to sleep. When he lay down near Kate, he watched Jonga for a moment as he sat leafing through the few pages of his old wordless book. Finally, he let them lie in his lap, and he lowered his head and slept.

Chad could barely keep his eyes open, but he wanted to stay awake, still a little wary of the four with their spears. Still, they seemed to obey Jonga, who was clearly a new friend. Chad also wanted to keep an ear open for Dad and Kate, in case their breathing became worse or they had some sort of trouble in the night. What if they awoke to see a Braza sitting by the fire, or four spearmen surrounding them?

But as much as he wanted to stay awake, Chad couldn't. He hoped and prayed they would be spotted at dawn from the air, and now, with a blazing fire going, they would be seen easily. The day's demands caught up with him and his body shut down. Never had he done so much in so short a time. Soon, Chad's whole world fell silent, and he was out cold.

Chad awoke with a start, squinting against the first sliver of the sun casting a pale yellow on the horizon. Kate had grabbed his collar and pulled. "Chad!" she whispered frantically. "The cannibals!"

Chad was stiff and sore and could hardly move, but he smiled and looked around. The four guardians were seated, their spears tilted toward the sky, dozing. Jonga lay on his side next to the dying embers of the fire.

"They're friends," Chad whispered, and quickly told her the whole story.

She smiled. "Tell Dad."

Chad slowly rose, trying not to groan aloud and wake anyone. Dad was in the same position as the night before, though his breathing seemed easier. "I think we should let him sleep. I want to make the fire bigger, though. I want the rescue planes to see us right away."

Chad stood and stretched. His ankles and knees were swollen, and his neck hurt no matter which way he turned his head. "Do you need this?" he asked Kate, picking up one of Dr. Howlett's shirts. She shook her head. Chad moved into the underbrush at the base of the mountain and used the shirt as a basket, loading it with more kindling and bigger sticks.

When Chad returned, the Brazas were rising. They looked puzzled that Chad would want a bigger fire, now that the sun was coming up. He didn't know how to explain it.

"Ah loo, Chahk," Jonga said, sitting up.

"Hello, Jonga," Chad said.

The old man smiled and looked at Kate.

"Kate," Chad said.

"Cake," Jonga said, but when Kate put out her hand, he would not shake it. He just nodded to her.

"Maybe they don't touch females or something," Chad said.

Jonga said something in his own dialect about the fire and looked as if he wanted to put it out. Chad hoped he would understand. He pointed to the sky, but not in the same way as when he had tried to indicate that Dr. Howlett was in heaven. This time he waved his finger back and forth and said, "Man-Man, Man-Man."

Could he possibly make Jonga understand that he was waiting for Mr. Coleman to arrive from the sky? From the look on Jonga's face, no. He and his friends stood in a cluster, as if wondering what to do next. Chad looked at his watch. In just a few minutes the search party would leave Bime. They would follow the same course Dad had flown. The fire would be easily spotted. Chad wondered how the Brazas would react.

Jonga's four companions, if Chad could understand them at all, appeared eager to get back to their own people. It had taken the one warrior forty-five minutes to go and get Jonga's wordless book, and so Chad calculated that their village must be a good twenty-minute hike away.

Jonga spoke quietly to the others, but immediately grew silent as the first search plane could be heard coming over the Great Dividing Range. They all looked up.

Ignoring his pain, Chad immediately began jumping and shouting. Kate struggled to balance on one foot, waving and squealing. Even Dad roused and tried to sit up.

"Can you move away from the fire, Dad?" Chad said. "I want to make it bigger."

Dad winced in pain as he pushed himself away with his left hand. Chad piled everything he had gathered onto the fire, and it began to roar and billow clouds of smoke.

"How'd you start the fire, Chad?" Dad said.

"Our new friends did it with their torch! And don't worry about them. I don't think they're still cannibals, if they ever were!"

"What new friends?" Dad asked.

Chad looked around while still waving at the small plane heading their way. The Brazas had disappeared. "Jonga!" he called. "Jonga! Man-Man! Treetzee!"

Dad forced himself to a sitting position and waved at the plane. "What in the world are you talking about?" he shouted.

"Long story!" Chad said. "Tell you later!"

The search plane followed the path of their tumble down the mountain; the pilot must have seen the metal sheets Chad put on the path. Next, he flew over the wreckage, turned in the direction of the grave, and then circled back around to where the little family waved and shouted. He dipped one wing and then the other to acknowledge he'd seen them. Then he flew back over the ridge.

"No way they can land a fixed-wing plane in here," Dad said. "Hope they can get a 'copter quick."

"How are you feeling?"

"Not good. I feel like my whole system is shot."

"They said something on the radio last night about a mission hospital in Angaruk."

"Good. That's not far from here."

By now, Kate was sitting again, pain etched in her face. Her foot looked terrible. "I can't wait to get out of here," she said.

Just then two small planes came over the rise. Kate started waving.

"No need to wave any more, honey" Dad said. "It's just the rest of the search party wanting to take a look." Both planes dipped their wings at the family and flew back. "Now, Chad, tell me what friends you were talking about."

As they scanned the horizon, waiting for the helicopter, Chad said, "Dad, you're not going to believe this..."

Chad told Dad all about the strange encounter with the Brazas, especially Jonga. It seemed all Dad could do was shake his head. Then, within half an hour, the whirring blades of a helicopter cut through the air. It landed between the plane wreckage and the fire, kicking up grass and dirt. The pilot and two searchers jumped from the chopper and ran to the family. Chad was thrilled to see that one of them was Dave Coleman. Chad told him quickly about Dr. Howlett and the injuries to Dad and Kate.

"Son, let's you and I stay put a while," Mr. Coleman shouted, "and leave them room to take your dad and sister to the mission hospital right away. That all right with you?"

Was it all right? It was perfect. He nodded and helped them load two stretchers onto the chopper. When it had lifted off, Chad said, "Mr. Coleman, your friend Jonga is not far away."

Mr. Coleman looked stunned. "What do you mean?"

"Jonga!" Chad shouted into the jungle. "Jonga! Treetzee! Man-Man!"

"Man-Man?" Mr. Coleman said. "Where did you hear that?"

"Dr. Howlett told us." And he told Mr. Coleman the story.

"He won't recognize me," Mr. Coleman said. "But I don't suppose I'd recognize him either."

"They're probably afraid of the helicopter." Chad said. "But they spent the night with us."

"And they ran off when the first plane few over?"

Chad nodded.

"Then you're right. They're probably not far away." He turned and made a megaphone of his hands. "Jonga! Shaka, Jonga. Treetzee!"

From the underbrush at the base of the mountain came the old man. If the others were there, they hung back out of sight. "Ah loo, Man-Man," Jonga said softly, and the veteran missionary hurried to him.

They shook hands at the wrist, and they tried to talk with the little bit each knew of the other's language. Mr. Coleman tried to explain who Chad was, and Jonga said, "Chahk and Cake."

Chad nodded.

Dave Coleman and Jonga spoke for several minutes and shook hands again. When Jonga retreated into the jungle, Mr. Coleman turned to Chad.

"Jonga accepted our message," he said. "With just that little knowledge of the wordless book and what we had told him those many years ago, he believed. He says a few other Brazas also believe, and the whole tribe is more peaceful and no longer cannibalistic. But it sounds like Jonga is basically an outcast. He still has his wordless book, and he wants me to come back."

When the helicopter returned, only the pilot was aboard. "I'm afraid this will be an unpleasant ride," Mr. Coleman said. "We need to take Doc Howlett's body with us. We have a bag for it."

Chad waited on the chopper while the pilot and Mr. Coleman dug up the body and loaded it. It was strange to ride to the mission hospital with the body of a man he had known, but he supposed no stranger than having had to bury him in the first place.

"You'd make quite a missionary, son," Mr. Coleman said as he climbed aboard. "It takes a man to do what you did. A real man. You saved your dad and sister's lives, you know."

"I guess."

"No guessing about it. It's clear God was with you, and you can be proud of what you did."

Chad was embarrassed and turned to study the scenery below. He saw the Indonesian mountain jungles with a whole new eye as they flew toward Angaruk. He would never forget this place.

Epilogue

I t was bitterly cold the first week of school in Mukluk, but there was not enough snow for the traditional daily snowball fight. Still, when Chad headed out for recess with his now seventh-grade classmates, he suspected the eighth graders were planning something. And Rusty Testor was looking right at Chad as he whispered to his friends.

"Let's play Chicken!" Rusty shouted suddenly, suggesting the one game Chad had always hated even more than the snowball fight. In Chicken, the two teams locked arms and lined up facing each other about two feet apart, arms locked. One boy would be chosen from each team and these two entered the narrow space between the teams from opposite ends. The first one to get to the other end won that round, but the only way to get there was to go through, or over, your opponent. You could tackle him, knock him over, climb over him, whatever you wanted. But you had to scramble past him to the other end before he got up and raced to his end. Teammates were supposed to keep their arms locked, but they could "help out" with their knees and feet.

Chad had been knocked around pretty well in Chicken in the past. Usually he had tried to squeeze by his opponent. That proved he was the Chicken, and he nearly always got tripped or blasted to the ground.

Today, though, he looked forward to the game. He had enjoyed the instant popularity that came with the newspaper article about his family's adventures in Indonesia, especially when it came out that he was a hero.

"You won't have any cigarette lighter or plane battery to protect you here," Rusty taunted Chad as the teams lined up. The big boy sauntered to one end of the chute of seventh graders. "I'm first, you wimps. Who dares?"

In the past, only two of Chad's friends dared face Rusty, and they always lost. But today, Chad beat them to it. He quickly unlocked arms and jogged to one end without a word. His friends looked at each other in surprise. The eighth graders laughed. Rusty said, "Oh, goody! Jungle boy!"

Rusty must have forgotten the rules to this game. Because once both players were lined up at either end, they could begin without notice, and before Rusty could even plant himself or start moving, Chad rushed forward. Rusty tensed at the last instant, unable to even take a step before Chad lowered his head and plowed into his stomach. Chad heard a great whoosh of air gush from the bigger boy as he drove him to the ground and scrambled over him. Rusty somersaulted backward, and the first round was over that quick.

Chad expected cries of "No fair!" or "I wasn't ready!" He half expected Rusty to come up swinging. But the redhead lay on the ground, moaning and gasping. "I can't breathe!" he mouthed, terror in his eyes. The teams separated and surrounded him.

"We'd better get some help," someone said.

"Nice goin', Michaels. You hurt him."

"I didn't mean to," Chad said, "and we don't need help. He just got the wind knocked out of him. I must've got him in mid-breath."

"Well, do something!"

Rusty looked panicky as Chad knelt over him. "Lie on your back! Now!"

Pale and grimacing, Rusty obeyed.

"Lift your knees to your chest!"

When Rusty brought his legs up, Chad straddled him and pushed slowly on his shins, he put slight pressure on his chest and then let up, which compressed and released Rusty's lungs. Suddenly the color returned to Rusty's cheeks and he looked relieved. He rolled to his side and sighed. "Thanks, man," he said. "I thought I was gonna die."

"Sorry," Chad said.

"Are you kiddin'? That was great! You reminded me of me!"

The scare made the other guys lose interest in Chicken for the rest of that recess. As they drifted away, Rusty remained on the ground. Chad didn't know whether to stay or leave. He started to move away, but Rusty spoke.

"You really scared those cannibals with a lighter and shocked one of 'em with a battery?"

Chad nodded. "We're not sure they were really cannibals, you know."

"Yeah, but still—"

They were silent for an awkward moment. "How's your dad doing?"

"Better. He's off the crutches and gets rid of the cane soon. Should be good as new."

"That's good."

Chad could hardly believe his ears. He was having an actual conversation with his enemy. Rusty struggled to his feet and brushed himself off. As they headed back toward the school building, he said, "You know, my cousin was in your mom's

Sunday school class last year…"

Chad continued to walk in silence.

"I'm sorry if you don't want to talk about her," Rusty spoke quietly.

"No, I love talking about her. Your cousin, huh?"

"Yeah, she thinks your mom was really cool."

Chad nodded. "She's right."

"She keeps trying to get me to come to your church."

Chad shrugged. "Any time. You might like it."

"Ah, I don't know. I've got an image, you know."

Chad snorted and chuckled. "Until today."

Rusty looked at him and grinned. Chad tried to conceal it but was nearly in shock. He didn't know exactly what it was that happened between the end of the last school year and the beginning of this one, but it was as if everything had transformed overnight. Was Rusty a different person? Or had Chad himself changed so much that everyone else just seemed different?

As Dad was saying good night that evening, Chad talked with him longer than he had for months. He told Dad what had happened that day.

"So no more calling yourself a wimp?" Dad said.

"I guess not."

"Still mad at God?"

Chad shook his head. "I still don't understand, though. I don't really see why Mom had to die, and I feel guilty because I'm not sure it is worth it just because some people became Christians at her funeral."

"Chad…" Dad settled himself on the edge of the bed.

"You've been through things that no one your age should have to endure. And I'm not going to sit here and tell you that you'll ever get over your mom's death. It will affect you for the rest of your life. And we may never know all the reasons why God allowed it. Or even why we crashed last summer in the jungle. But it's our job to trust Him, to look for the good that comes from bad. We can let these things tear us up, or we can grow and become what He wants us to be. You proved in the jungle that you could do what you had to do. You've got to face losing Mom the same way you faced those dangers."

Chad nodded. It wouldn't be easy, but he knew Dad was right. He could let circumstances rule his life or he could react to them in a way that made his whole life seem different. He remembered he let Rusty Testor pummel him with snowballs, or when he let bitterness and grief over Mom's death overwhelm him, or when he thought about giving up in the jungle—all those times his life seemed almost worthless. But when he faced himself and danger and even his enemy, he saw how different life could be.

Dad swatted Chad on the leg. "And I promise not to get you into any more situations where your life is at risk."

"Are you kidding?" Chad said. "That was the best part!"

"You're ready for another assignment then?" Dad pulled a long white envelope from his pocket.

"What do you mean?"

"Kate!" Dad called. "Can you come in here for a second?"

Kate padded in, ready for bed. She looked puzzled.

Dad pulled out a letter he had received that day from a couple in Washington State. "They're having trouble with the government in a new South American republic, and they want me to fly them in with supplies for a children's relief organization."

Chad and Kate looked at each other and rolled their eyes. "Here we go again," they said in unison.